Fearless Warrior

Fearless Warrior

A Gunner's Mate on the Beach at Guadalcanal

by Bill Kennedy

with a foreword by
VICE ADMIRAL GORDON R. NAGLER
US NAVY (RET.)

McFarland & Company, Inc., Publishers
Jefferson, North Carolina, and London

British Library Cataloguing-in-Publication data are available

Library of Congress Cataloguing-in-Publication Data

Kennedy, Bill, 1923–
    Fearless warrior : a gunner's mate on the beach at
Guadalcanal / by Bill Kennedy.
      p. cm.
    ISBN 0-89950-606-2 (lib. bind. : 50# alk. paper) ∞
    1. World War, 1939–1945 – Campaigns – Solomon Islands. 2. World
War, 1939–1945 – Naval operations, American. 3. Guadalcanal Island
(Solomon Islands), Battle of, 1942–1943. 4. World War, 1939–1945 –
Personal narratives, American. 5. Kennedy, Bill, 1923– .
I. Title.
D767.98.K46   1991
940.54'26 – dc20   90-53605
                                                   CIP

Manufactured in the United States of America

McFarland & Company, Inc., Publishers
  Box 611, Jefferson, North Carolina 28640

To Jerry,
the pretty girl I met at Texas Tech

Acknowledgments

B efore I could put this tale in chronological order, I searched the public library for reference books about the campaign in the Solomons and the war in the Southwest Pacific in those early days. I read and used material gleaned from several good books. The big surprise came when I was unable to find a source that had anything of substance to say about the sailors who manned the landing craft which took the Marines ashore and then remained to set up the Naval Operating Base. These sailors were also instrumental in getting the cargo off the ships and on the beach, and they later hauled the Marine raiding parties up and down the beach when they made sorties behind the Japanese lines. Perhaps such records do exist, but I was unable to locate them. All I found were simple statements to the effect that "the Marines stepped on each other's hands going down the rope ladders to get in the landing craft..." and "the flotilla of landing craft loaded with Marines circled until given the command to go ashore..." There was much more to it than that, believe me!

Two books, in particular, were most helpful: Time-Life Books' edition of *Island Fighting,* and *Pacific Onslaught* by Ballentine Books, Inc. I also used *Guadalcanal Remembered* by Herbert Merillat. Many of my remembered experiences in those early days were disjointed until I researched material for this tale. I can now, at last, associate my being in a certain place or participating in a certain event because I now have most of those events dated and in their proper perspective.

There was another book which appeared to be historically accurate, but one I would not use because of its biased theology, a false theology for those who perceive God in his loving and compassionate nature. *Do It Again* was written by Marvin Harris; he espouses the hypothesis that the United States was victorious in World War II only because *"God gave the victory by answering the prayers of Godly people back home."* The accuracy of events in this book is commended by Rear Admiral E. M. Eller (Ret.), Director of Naval History. Rather than finding this work scholarly, I found it offensive. Did 35,000,000 people die, some horribly and slowly, because somebody else failed to pray enough? I wonder what Mr. James would say to the survivors of the Holocaust? And what about our own who died in combat; did their loved ones back home let them down by not spending enough time in prayer? It seems that the easy way out is to look heavenward and blame God for our own human frailties. What a shame.

The least we can do is to be objective when we look back at the war in which so many lives were lost. God was not on "our side," nor was He on theirs, either. I think, rather, that God wept over the way His creatures sought to destroy one another.

Last, but by no means least, I want to thank my cousin, Emogene (now Gene Perry). Not only did she do a great job of proofing and editing the text, she was a deep well of ideas and encouragement.

Table of Contents

Foreword

I t has been my privilege to know Bill Kennedy for the past 35 years. From 1956 to 1959 we were neighbors in Honolulu, Hawaii, at the time I was a young lieutenant on the staff of the Commander-in-Chief, U.S. Pacific Fleet at Pearl Harbor and Bill was running an insurance agency. When we first met, the war had been over for only 11 years, and although Bill was a successful young businessman, he still had a lot of the "old salt" in him. He told good sea stories and enjoyed people and parties—in that order. We became good friends and have remained so over the years even though we usually get to see each other only on special occasions.

Bill's story of the Solomon Island campaign through the eyes of a 19-year-old sailor is very realistic and sometimes quite graphic. Times of adversity usually bring Americans together as was the case with Bill and thousands of other young men who enlisted the day after the bombing of Pearl Harbor. His story of the events that followed has caught the spirit of the times; he has written a very readable book, one with which most of the veterans of the war can easily identify, regardless of where they served.

Great history books have been written about America's first offensive in the Southwest Pacific, but *Fearless Warrior* is the first I have seen that was written from the perspective of a 19-year-old gunner's mate. War histories written by military historians abound but this one is a first. In his tale about this part of the war, Bill does not pull any punches; he tells the good with the bad, and he is the first to admit that he was no angel. We see him as an ordinary young man from Texas, one who was forced to grow up in a hurry. He was also one of the lucky ones who survived the war but brought home the dregs of jungle rot, malaria, and dengue along with a firsthand knowledge of the price we sometimes have to pay to preserve our freedom. He brings the book to its logical ending with his medical discharge in November of 1943. At that time, his 6'4" frame carried only 118 pounds.

What Bill chose *not* to write about is also quite interesting. This is especially true after you get to know him by reading his book. In 1966, as a successful 43-year-old businessman, he chose to forgo the trappings of a successful business career in an effort to find that "missing link" that would help him put his life in its proper perspective. He enrolled in Berkeley Divinity School at Yale University and was ordained to the priesthood in the Episcopal Church in 1969. I was fortunate to hear him preach his first sermon in Washington that year. Bill's business background helped him with the work he did in putting struggling parishes back on a firm foundation.

On a personal note, when our friendship began, Rick, our youngest, was only five years old. A few years ago, he asked Bill to come to Savannah to officiate at his wedding.

The Reverend Bill Kennedy retired from the Episcopal church in 1989 — but not for long. His bishop asked him to "take over the reins of this small rural parish..." until a suitable replacement could be called. A year later, he was still there exercising the same zeal and enthusiasm that has always been the way he works.

Bill Kennedy is a dedicated American and a great Christian, a man who I am proud to have as a friend. I hope you enjoy his collection of sea stories as much as I did.

> Gordon R. Nagler
> Vice Admiral
> U.S. Navy (Retired)

Preface

Mine was a very small part in a very big war, a war that was to become the biggest and deadliest in the history of mankind. Global in scope, it produced the longest battle lines, and it cost more than all our previous wars combined. Before it came to an end, more than 35,000,000 people worldwide, the majority of whom were not in uniform, would be killed. When peace finally came, the United States still had more than 11,000,000 men and women in uniform.

As my sons were growing up, they loved to listen to "what Dad did in the war." After they were grown, my eldest son kept after me to "put some of these stories in writing. Someday you'll be dead and all those great stories will be lost." That is the purpose of this writing—which began as a few disjointed stories but ended being my war memoir.

I was called a "Higgins Boat Sailor" because all but a few days of my overseas service were ashore, hauling Marines off of and onto ships and in and out of strikes behind enemy lines, and unloading the ships that brought us more guns, ammunition, aviation gasoline, and rations—and more replacements. Ashore, we were the Naval Operating Base.

During my tour in the Solomon Islands, we were a part of the ancillary force of the First Marine Division, Reinforced. I am as proud as any Marine of the Presidential Unit Citation awarded me for my part in that campaign.

Bill Kennedy

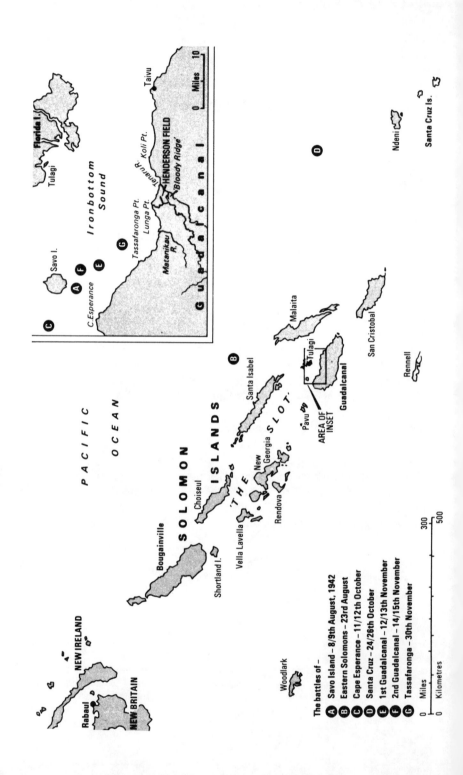

The battles of –
Ⓐ Savo Island – 8/9th August, 1942
Ⓑ Eastern Solomons – 23rd August
Ⓒ Cape Esperance – 11/12th October
Ⓓ Santa Cruz – 24/26th October
Ⓔ 1st Guadalcanal – 12/13th November
Ⓕ 2nd Guadalcanal – 14/15th November
Ⓖ Tassafaronga – 30th November

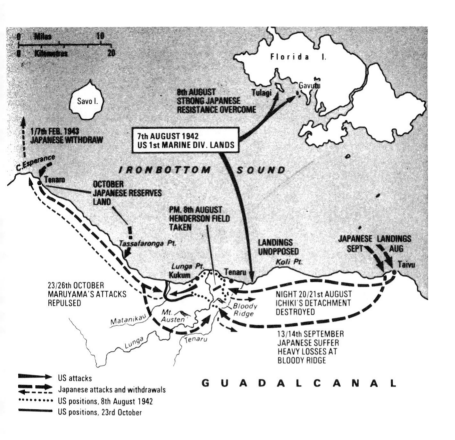

Miles 0 ___ 10
Kilometres 0 ___ 20

Florida I.

Savo I.

8th AUGUST
STRONG JAPANESE
RESISTANCE OVERCOME

Tulagi · Gavutu

7th AUGUST 1942
US 1st MARINE DIV. LANDS

1/7th FEB. 1943
JAPANESE WITHDRAW

C.Esperance

Tenaro

IRONBOTTOM SOUND

OCTOBER
JAPANESE RESERVES
LAND

PM. 8th AUGUST
HENDERSON FIELD
TAKEN

Tassafaronga Pt.

LANDINGS
UNOPPOSED

Koli Pt.

JAPANESE LANDINGS
SEPT   AUG

Taivu

Lunga Pt.
Kukum

Tenaru

23/26th OCTOBER
MARUYAMA'S ATTACKS
REPULSED

Matanikau

Mt.
Austen

Bloody
Ridge

Lunga

Tenaru

NIGHT 20/21st AUGUST
ICHIKI'S DETACHMENT
DESTROYED

13/14th SEPTEMBER
JAPANESE SUFFER
HEAVY LOSSES AT
BLOODY RIDGE

US attacks
Japanese attacks and withdrawals
US positions, 8th August 1942
US positions, 23rd October

GUADALCANAL

**Opposite: Events in the Solomon Islands, August 7–November 30, 1942.
Above: The American Landing on Guadalcanal. (Maps are from _Pacific
Onslaught_ by Paul Kennedy, copyright © 1972 by Ballantine Books, a Division of Random House, Inc.)**

The Patriot

The Japanese bombed Pearl Harbor on the morning of December 7, 1941. I enlisted in the United States Navy on the morning of December 8, 1941, before President Franklin Delano Roosevelt proclaimed to the world a declaration of war.

For the record, I must confess that my immediate response to our national emergency did not come from patriotic zeal nor some other high-sounding principle. I hinted at sometime like patriotism to my young sons when we were watching a war movie or talking about "what Daddy did" in the war. Actually, my reason for the immediate enlistment was one of expediency: I very simply did not want to miss out on the opportunity of fighting in a war! I don't know about the rest of the country, but nobody in west Texas (at least, nobody that I knew) took the Japanese very seriously. Japan was a little-bitty country on the other side of the world that made cheap toys, copied or stole other countries' technology, and manufactured other stuff that we could buy if we wanted to go third-class; all their products, we thought, were inferior. We not only thought that the Japanese people were inferior to us Americans, we thought Japan was foolish to have attacked the big, powerful United States (who, we didn't dare admit, had been brought to her knees by the Great Depression of the '30s). A war with the United States couldn't last long, we thought, but while it did last, I wanted a piece of the action.

*   *   *

Sunday mornings where I grew up were "Church mornings"; just about everybody went to church, not because it was expected, but because that was what nearly everybody did during the Depression. Nobody "got religion" in our socio-economic society, we were born with religion! I missed going to church that particular Sunday morning because there was a dance at the Hilton Hotel on Saturday night, the 6th, and I was tired after working all day in the men's clothing store then dancing until midnight. Funny thing about those

1

dances, they always ended right on the stroke of midnight with the orchestra playing "Good Night, Sweetheart." They not only ended precisely at 12 A.M., but our dates had to be home by 1 A.M. — which usually left us with a terrible decision: We could go to the drive-in for Cokes and french fries, or we could park on a certain side street and smooch for about 45 minutes. My date and I decided to smooch that night, so all the fellows met later for the Cokes and fries. Must have been close to 2 A.M. before I got home. I don't even remember turning the old Big Ben alarm clock off the next morning, so it was afternoon before I heard the news about Pearl Harbor.

*   *   *

The guys I ran around with got together that afternoon and ended up in a big corner booth at Wylie's Drug Store; we listened to the radio and ate hamburgers. In twos and threes, other kids from the high school drifted in and joined us in that corner. It wasn't long until there were about 20 of us there. We were all excited about the war and talked about what we'd like to do. Eventually, the majority of the males present decided that we would join the Marine Corps immediately so we could see some real action real fast. Many people thought the war would be over in six months; others thought it might last as long as a year. Whatever, we wanted to get in on it before it was too late.

In retrospect, "getting in on the action" was an excuse, not the real reason. It was not until I was a mature adult that I finally admitted to myself that I was ready to go to almost any extreme to get away from home — to get as far away as I possibly could from my mother. Why? Because I was an abused child, physically and psychologically. Even now when I think about my childhood, I'm embarrassed for my mother because of the way she mistreated me. She hated me from the day I was born (which I'm sure was subconscious) because I was not a girl, among other things. Just take a look at the name given on my birth certificate: "Billie." Feminine. No middle name. I remember her saying, many times, how disappointed she was because I was not born a girl, "so that ours would be an ideal-sized family, two boys and two girls."

One of my earliest memories, at about age three, was her whipping me with a thin willow switch on my bare legs and buttocks — she enjoyed it, always. It was usually two or three days before the marks healed and disappeared. I remember once (at about that age) when she and her sister, my Aunt Bo, swapped children to "switch." I suppose we had misbehaved, so mother beat my cousin Emogene while Aunt Bo whipped me.

I guess maybe that "switch-off" was the bond that made Gene and me friends for life, despite our being cousins. Gene (as she was soon to be called) had every reason to steer clear of me after I shot her in the face with that 22-caliber pistol. It was an accident, of course, and could have been tragic but, thanks be to God, it wasn't. Gene was three; I was four. Her brothers, George and Frank, were about 16 and 13 years old and, at that time, were blank-pistol buffs—which was then the fad. No real bullets, but they enjoyed shooting blanks. When they heard we were coming over for the day, they hid their gun in a corner under the bed where I found it less than an hour after we walked in the door.

I'll never forget what happened: Gene was sitting on the floor playing with some empty spools.

"Stick 'em up."

She ignored me and continued to play.

"Stick 'em up or I'm gonna shoot you."

She continued playing so I pulled the trigger. BLAM! I was standing less than three feet from her when the gun fired—which was fortunate, under the circumstances. The blast of powder hit Gene squarely on the right cheek about two inches under the eye. The wound bled at the time but it was not a serious wound except that the powder blast tatooed a black spot on her cheek, about the size of a quarter, a mark that she was to wear for the next 30 years. In high school, I once heard someone ask her about that black spot.

"How did you get that mark?"

"My cousin Bill shot me." No elaboration.

By the time she went to college, the spot had begun to absorb and eventually disappeared, but it took a full generation to do so. Her grown children still remember it—and I certainly do!

Her life was charmed at the moment I pulled the trigger—and so was mine. The black spot itself was not easy for either of us to live with, but what if there had been a hard bullet in the chamber of that pistol and I had blown her head off?

*   *   *

By the time I was six or seven, mother graduated me from the willow switch to what she called "The Quirt." Actually, what she used was what the old British Navy called a "cat-o'-nine-tails." I still remember that damnable thing—and I remember it vividly. For a handle, it had a round wooden shaft an inch or so in diameter and about five inches long with a leather strap attached that looped around the wrist; attached to the other end of the shaft were nine thin leather strips about a foot-and-a-half long and probably a quarter-inch wide, that were split up from the ends about six inches, with each of the 18 ends tied into a hard knot. It made the "business end" of the Quirt an almost lethal weapon; one whack from it was tantamount to receiving 18 lashes! The Quirt was my transition from being whipped to being beaten. For the rest of my life I would remember 18 hard leather knots biting my legs, buttocks, or back. Sometimes she brought the blood, but usually it was bruises — long, thin bruises with big bruises about the size of a nickel at the end where the knot bit into the flesh. They were reddish welts, at first, but later turned blue and purple and green. Brutal. I was perhaps 13 years old, maybe older, the last time I got The Quirt. I don't know what happened to it, but it — and she — left me with some permanent damage. You can't see it, but it's there.

The other reason she didn't like me was because I did not measure up to my older brothers (17 and 15 years older) and my sister (7 years older). I was led to believe that I wasn't very smart — and I was always into some kind of mischief. Nothing ever really bad, but I responded easily and quickly to whatever temptation was at hand. If my mother wouldn't recognize my attributes, then I made damn sure that I was recognized for something else.

During the 1920s, for the first three or four years of my public schooling, the boys all wore short pants except in the winter. I was grateful when the cold weather came and I could wear overalls or knickers with long stockings because they covered my bruises. Short-pant weather was embarrassing to me because my classmates could see the marks of what a bad person I was. If that sort of thing happened in today's society, the school or a neighbor or somebody would call the police and I would be placed in a foster home. If it hadn't been for my dad, I don't think I could have made it. He was a gentle giant of a man, completely dominated by my mother. I never knew why he took the stuff from her that he did. Maybe it was because he was 20 years older than she was; maybe he had guilt feelings about his mercantile business in west Texas failing in the late twenties. Whatever, for some reason he did take it. He had the patience of Job and I loved him dearly.

*   *   *

Meanwhile, back to Pearl Harbor Day...

There was one small problem with my enlistment — but I didn't let it stand in my way: I was 18 years old and had not yet graduated from high school. If the truth is to be fully known, I was not a good student. Actually, I was a lousy student. (In all probability, the sub-par scholastic performance was my way of striking back for the abuse I got at home.) I was supposed to have graduated from Lubbock High School in June of 1941 but did not because I didn't have a C average. I studied very little in school and did as little homework as I could get by with — and many times none at all. The extra semester or two before graduation was meant to bring my grade-point average up and to give me the opportunity of retaking the second semester of a required algebra course that I had flunked the year before. Unfortunately, things didn't work out that way.

In addition to my being a poor student, I could, when the occasion arose, be somewhat of a smart-ass. An occasion of that sort did present itself early in that extra semester, probably in October of 1941; it was in Mr. Groves' algebra class. It happened like this: "Pop" Groves was sitting on a desk in the corner of the classroom talking to a group of students. I did not join in the discussion mainly because I didn't know what they were talking about. They were talking algebra, but it might well have been Greek for all I understood. Instead of participating, I cleaned out my notebook, took all the discarded pieces of paper and wadded them into a ball about the size of a cantaloupe. When I got up to go to the wastebasket — in front of where the teacher was sitting — Mr. Groves lowered his head and glared at me over the tops of his glasses and pointing, said, "Sit down." I did, but before I did I turned around and tossed the wad of paper back over my shoulder halfway across the room in the direction of the wastepaper basket. I'm convinced that if I had missed the basket, all I would have gotten would have been ten days in detention hall. But I didn't miss; that big wad plunked right into the center of the wastebasket. Everybody laughed except Mr. Groves — and me; I knew I was in trouble. Again looking over the top of his glasses at me, he pointed to the door and said, "Out. Get out of my class."

No sweat. All I had to do was go to the office and get rescheduled into another algebra class. Problem was, there was not another class that semester. Another problem was that Mr. Groves' action was final. No amount of pleading or sweet talk swayed him. I was definitely out of his class. (And I deserved what I got.) At the end of the semester, I would still lack that one-half credit in algebra. No graduation until June, 1942.

*   *   *

Meanwhile, back to the war...

That Sunday afternoon of December 7th, the reason we decided—my buddies and I—that the Marine Corps was *the* elite service, was because it had classier uniforms, more opportunity to earn medals, more glamour, and we would probably be in combat sooner—all very important propaganda that was crucial to the part we would play in the war effort. We agreed, all five of us, that we would meet and "sign up" at the recruiting station in the Post Office Building at 9 A.M. the next morning, December 8th. And we did, all of us except Chuck Hawkins; he was late. When we arrived at the recruiting office that morning, there were already about 50 guys lined up at the Marine Corps recruiter's door. Across the hall, at the Navy Recruiting Station, there were only three guys so we all got in the shorter line—that is, all except Chuck. When he arrived just a little late, he didn't see us in the Marine Corps line, so he assumed we had backed out. He got in line and enlisted in the Marines while we were across the hall joining the Navy. Our enlistment dates show December 8th, but we were given until December 25th to report for active duty.

We were all heroes, of course, rushing down like that to fight for our country to save democracy and all those other high-sounding phrases. The teachers at the high school were very understanding (I didn't know why some of them cried. Were theirs the tears of joy at my departure from their classrooms?) but they gave me my final exams the week before the Christmas holiday began. I passed 'em all, brought my grade-point average up, but did not graduate because of that blind, lucky shot backward over my shoulder in that algebra class. (If I had done that in the gym class, I would have been considered a jock, which was a big compliment for a cheer-leader.)

We reported for active duty at 9 P.M. on Christmas night at the Santa Fe railroad depot in time to catch the daily train for Dallas where we were to report to the main Navy Recruiting Station for further transfer to boot camp in San Diego, California. We were having a mild winter in Texas, so everyone took a minimum of clothing: an extra shirt, a change of underwear, and an extra pair of socks. I wore a lightweight cotton jacket because I didn't want to be encumbered with too many clothes. What we took with us we would give to the Salvation Army once we were in uniform — which we expected to be in three or four days.

As with most things military, it didn't work that way; we learned our first military lesson: Hurry up and wait. We spent the next ten days in Dallas at the YMCA, doing nothing but hanging around the Y and checking in every morning to see if our orders for the California boot camp had come through. We didn't come prepared to be civilians very long, so everyone had to hand-wash some of his clothing every night and then iron shirts or pants the next morning with a borrowed iron, one that came from a second-floor walk-up hotel in the next block, on a short street named South Akard. We were young and somewhat naive and sure didn't know that the hotel was actually a whorehouse until the day we departed for boot camp. Actually, it was not until then that we learned that all those second story walk-up hotels on South Akard were whorehouses — and there were a bunch of them. This new-found knowledge didn't really matter because we had very little money when we arrived in Dallas and were pretty near broke when our orders finally came through. Besides, we were still living in the era of the Great Depression at that time and nobody had budgeted two bucks for that kind of extracurricular activity. We heard later that the guys going through the recruiting stations in Dallas got a one dollar discount on their "visits" for a few months, but that burst of patriotism came after we had shipped out. Also a note of interest concerning wartime pleasures of the flesh: The two-dollar price everywhere soon escalated to three dollars, then four, and was up to five bucks by the end of the war. My economics professor at The University of Texas said that the price of nookie was a prime indicator in the military wartime cost-of-living index.

To make the idleness even worse, a blizzard blew in a couple of days after we arrived, so we didn't leave the warmth of the YMCA except to go to the hamburger joint across the street. It was ten cents for hamburgers but two bits for a burger, fries, a Coke, and a piece of day-old pie if they had it. All with chow chits issued by the Navy recruiter. Got monotonous after a while, bacon and eggs and hamburgers and fries.

Boot Camp

The orders finally came—to go to Chicago, of all places! We were to go to the Naval Training Center at Great Lakes, Illinois, for physicals and uniforms, then on to the Recruit depot there for boot camp.

Back on the train, it was a two-day journey to Chicago. The trip was a nightmare even though we did eat pretty good meals in the Pullman Diner—and we had sleepers, too. The train didn't miss a stop at a single jerk-water town and hit its top speed—45 miles per hour—only twice during the trip. It was ten degrees the night we arrived at the Chicago terminal and colder still when the bus got us to the receiving station at Great Lakes. We were all cold, hungry, and exhausted when they marched us about a quarter of a mile through the snow to the mess hall. I've never been very picky about food but what the Navy called a sandwich that night was two hunks of bread with a dab of mayonnaise smeared on one side and a small dab of ham, no more than an ounce or so, hidden somewhere in the middle. The march to and from in the ice-cold weather was worth it for the cups of the best-tasting hot, scalding coffee I have ever had. That's one place the Navy excelled; I never had a bad cup of coffee.

Because we were newly arrived recruits, they let us sleep in (late, that is) the next morning; reveille, for us, did not sound until 6 A.M. Lordy mercy, count your blessings! No towels, so we couldn't shower, but we did shave, dried our hands and faces on our shirt tails or big balls of rolled-up toilet paper, brushed our teeth, then fell in for the icy march back to the chow hall for breakfast.

The Navy called it breakfast—but it sure as hell wasn't like any breakfast anybody ever saw in west Texas. At first, I thought it was a mistake or maybe some kind of a joke, one like they play on you when you're initiated into a club or something. Some of us giggled and said something to the mess cooks in the serving line, but they just looked at us like we were nonpersons and kept right on dishing out the chow. Here's the deal: For breakfast, there on that tray, was coffee (fine!), baked beans, cornbread, and an apple! It was no joke; it was a standard Navy breakfast menu, one that was served much

8

more often in the days ahead than the eggs we were accustomed to back home.

By 7:30 we were reassembled and marched in a different direction. (It didn't matter which direction because we didn't have the slightest idea where we were going or what was about to happen to us.) The building we were headed for was a pretty good distance away and we were so lightly dressed that the sailor in charge made us double-time to this single-story, extra-long building. There was a red cross on the door and a stenciled sign that said "RECEIVING." And we were received by a pot-bellied hospital corpsman who spoke in a high-pitched voice. He told us to line up, take off our clothes, and place them in a neat pile in front of us. This we did and thus began the post-induction medical examination, and it was thorough. When they said, "Bend over and spread your cheeks," I was glad to see that the guy next to me from Lamesa, Texas, did not hook his fingers in the corners of his mouth the way he did at the pre-induction exam in Dallas.

*   *   *

Funny how some guys can't pass water into a little bottle in front of a bunch of strange people. Nothing to it; just dribble a little. Nobody watched because nobody really cared about something that routine. That was the last thing we had to do before passing through the double doors on the way to Supply for uniforms. When I came back a couple of hours later, fully dressed, to get my wallet and toilet articles from my pile of civvies, a couple of guys were still sitting there with glum looks on their faces, still naked, and still holding their empty specimen bottles. The corpsman in our combat outfit later said that some guys' bladders just freeze when they're on public display for a specimen and are so frozen that they eventually have to be catheterized. Guess I'm just insensitive; I can usually help nature along when the occasion demands but I've never had to try in front of more than 500 people. (A really large crowd might inhibit me.)

*   *   *

Issuing uniforms to recruits is a precision operation: Long counters on each side of the room with Supply Corps sailors on either side of the counters, one taking measurements and yelling sizes while the other pulls items off the shelves and plunks them down on the counter in front of us. I welcomed the order to put on my new skivvies (underwear). It was a little chilly, for one thing, and I wasn't accustomed to all that activity with 500 other bare-assed young men. Even though all men are created equal, I felt more comfortable with my skivvies on because some men are created more equal than others.

Before we went in for uniforms, scuttlebutt was that Supply looked at you and threw out clothing they thought would fit, and if it didn't all you had to do was trade around with other misfits until everyone had uniforms that didn't look too bad. Not so. Even fussy mothers couldn't have done better. After the Supply Corps sailor measured me very carefully, I had to put on each item then wait for a nod of approval from an old chief petty officer who was overseeing the operation. No Annapolis midshipman was ever outfitted with greater care. It was great; we all marched out of there suited out in the finest tradition of the United States Navy, I alone being the exception.

The last item of clothing was shoes. When my turn came, I stepped up on the platform and placed my foot in the measuring device. The sailor operating that thing made two or three quick adjustments, then looked up at me and said, "What size shoe do you wear?"

"Thirteen AAAA."

"Look, kid, the Navy don't have that kind of sizes. What other size can you wear?"

"That's all I've ever worn. Any other size wouldn't fit, would it?"

He called the Chief over and the Chief called over another sailor who left shortly and came back with a 20-year-old ensign, a guy not much older than me; we even had the same kind of peach fuzz on our chins. I couldn't hear what they were saying but I knew they were talking about me by the way they kept glancing back at me, like I was some kind of a freak from a sideshow. A decision was finally reached, I assumed, when one of the sailors left, went into a back room, and emerged with a pair of shoes. "Try these, Mac. They're the best the Navy can do." Wow, size 12 B. I put 'em on, laced them as tight as I could, then flapped around the room with the other guys as we finished up getting our Navy-issue clothing and bedding. There was at least a half-inch of space beteen the ball of my foot and the edge of the shoe. I felt I was walking like one of those circus clowns who wore big, oversized shoes that made flapping noises as they walked.

The last item to be issued was somewhat of a shock. Not the

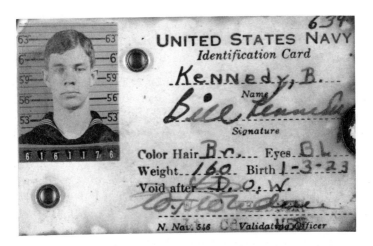

The author's Navy-issued Liberty card.

hammocks; they even looked a little like they might be a little fun. The last issue was a "Sea Bag," a tubular canvas affair about three feet tall and about 18 inches in diameter. Waterproofed canvas, it would probably have held about 20 gallons of liquid. The shocker came when they told us that all the clothing we had been issued that day had to be put in that one bag! I couldn't get my stuff in two of those bags, but nobody listened to our protests and nobody seemed concerned. Once outfitted, we went back to the receiving hall for our personal effects left in the neat little piles of civvies. Very few piles were sent home; most went to the Salvation Army.

One of the stops in that half-day uniform-issue process was for dog tags and ID cards. Unlike the ground troops who got two tags, the Navy issued only one, showing name, serial number, religious preference (C for Catholic, P for Protestant), and blood type. About the size of a half-dollar, they were flat on two sides and rounded on the ends. I was very proud of mine because this was the only thing the Navy had done thus far to rstore a little of my identity and individuality. We had a "group" look: same clothes, same hair-cuts, and no physical secrets. At least, I knew I was

BILL KENNEDY
464-11-76
P
A POSITIVE

One young guy looked at his newly issued status symbol and remarked, "Hey, how did they know I was a Presbyterian?"

*   *   *

The name on my dog tag was different from that on my birth certificate because I was able to get it changed when I was about ten years old. All my life I had lived with that girl's name. Billie. Young kids can be pretty cruel, you know. Since I had grown up in the same neighborhood, I was stuck with that female identification. I tried to get a nickname to stick but nobody wanted to call me Spud or whatever else struck my fancy at the time. I was always Billie with the lace on his drawers, and they teased me by saying that I played with dolls. My time came, though, when we moved to a new neighborhood and I was transferred to a new school! To my new friends in the neighborhood and at school, I said, "My name is Bill."

It worked, and it became legal (and binding) the following Easter. For some reason, my folks did not have me baptized as an infant. Why, I was never told. Easter baptisms were a big thing in the Methodist church in Lubbock so I unwittingly used that time to officially change my name. Near the close of the service, the candidates for baptism were told to come forward. My time came.

"What's your name?"

"Bill."

"What's your middle name?"

"I don't have one."

The district superintendent eyed me suspiciously because I had been going to church there all my life and he had known me as Billie since I was in diapers, but he went along with what I had said. He didn't dare pursue it there in front of that once-a-year standing-room-only congregation. Bending my head over that font, he took a handful of water and poured it over the crown of my sandy hair.

"Bill, I baptize you in the name of the Father, and of the Son, and of the Holy Ghost...."

That did it. I graduated, enlisted, married, and was ordained all in my Christian name.

*   *   *

Boot haircuts are high on the memory list for most boot trainees, but not for me. At least, not for the kind of haircut I got. I had always liked short hair so liked the idea of the almost-shaved head I knew I was going to have. Having worked for S&Q Clothiers for the past five years (after school, weekends, and summers), my boss insisted on what he deemed "presentable and acceptable" hair styles, so that was what I expected of the Navy—and that's the way my hair was cut. Pat Wyman worked for S&Q also, but the presentable and acceptable kind of coiffure was no problem to him—as a civilian. While we worked at S&Q, Pat had the best looking head of hair I have ever seen on a man. (One of his dates once said to me, "His hair is gorgeous; it's the kind any woman would kill for!") He wore it just a little longer than most of us; it was black, thick, wavy, and parted in the middle. In all the years I had known him, Pat never once looked like he needed a haircut and he never once looked like he had just come from a barbershop.

Boot haircuts always bring guffaws and kidding, but nothing like Pat got. When he sat down in the barber chair, there must have been 30 guys crowding that little barber shop. (The boots didn't need a big barber shop; the normal GI "recruit cut" took only 67 seconds to complete.) I can imagine how Samson must have felt after Delilah had exercised her tonsorial artistry on him because Pat probably looked and felt very much the same. To say that Pat was forlorn would be an understatement, and all the kidding from the guys sure didn't do anything to help his morale. Pat and I had been friends for several years, so I knew him well and I felt very sorry for the poor guy. Until it grew out, that boot camp haircut changed not only Pat's appearance but his personality. Fortunately, both came back as each grew in proportion to the other, but for a while there I had trouble recognizing Pat in a crowd.

*   *   *

After five hours in the Dispensary and Supply, we all straggled back to the barracks. We were not in formation and we had more gear in our arms than it was humanly possible to carry at one time. We had four pairs of shorts, four T-shirts, four pairs of black socks, three pairs of white socks, two pairs of Navy blue wool pants (13-button front), two undress blue jumpers, one dress blue jumper, two undress white jumpers, two white pants (button fly), two white hats, one dress blue hat, one watch camp, two dungaree shirts, two dungaree pants, one dungaree jacket, one pea jacket, two small bath towels, one mattress, one mattress cover, one pillow and pillowcase, one ditty bag, and one sea bag. The unbelievable part is that *all* of the clothing except the pea jacket had to fit in the sea bag and the mattress, mattress cover, and pillow had to be tied together in such a manner as to wrap around the sea bag, lengthwise, and be carried over the shoulder as one bundle! It can be done; I did it.

Once back in the barracks, there were some salty old sailors assigned to show us how each item had to be rolled then tied and stowed in the bag, but not before we were given stencils and showed how to stencil and where to stencil our names on every single thing that was issued to us, both Navy blues and whites. After the stenciling was done and dry, our instructors were very thorough and patient in showing us how each item had to be folded a very certain way, then rolled, and then tied. When we were finished, hours later, not only did everything fit, but if jackets and pants (wool dress stuff and white cotton dress stuff) were properly rolled and tied, they could stay in the sea bag for months at a time and still be ready for wear once untied — looking like they had just been pressed by the base tailor. This is truly one of the mysteries of the sea! We were also taught that a properly packed sea bag and hammock would float and support a normal sized man for as long as four hours. I never had to try it, but it was a comfort to know.

*   *   *

Next morning after reveille, we were all packed and ready to be transported, bag and baggage, over to the Recruit Depot on the other side of the base to begin our 12 weeks of intense boot training. We marched in formation (if you could call it that) to the chow hall and then back to the transit barracks. The old chief came in shortly and told us to show our bags on the truck, then board the bus; we were on our way to boot camp — at Navy Pier in Chicago! The chief told us that Great Lakes and San Diego, the Navy's only two boot camps, were full and that recruits were waiting in YMCA facilities all over the country. Navy Pier was the first of many auxiliary boot camps to be opened.

The long convoy of buses and trucks took the better part of three hours to make it from Great Lakes to downtown Chicago. The traffic was heavy and the streets were treacherous with the ice and snow. Nighttime temperatures the two nights we had been aboard at Great lakes were near zero and the daytime highs were in the low teens — and the weather stayed in that range, with intermittent show, for all of January, 1942.

Navy Pier was the largest building under one roof that I had ever seen; it was one big warehouse-type building. It extended a good mile, I imagine, out into the lake. No rooms, partitions, dividers, or anything except for the head (that's a john to a non-sailor). Someone said that our contingent of about 5,000 trainees were the first to utilize that giant facility since the beginning of the Great Depression. I never found out what the Pier had been used for originally. It was obviously built to house personnel, not living facilities to make you feel like you were at home, but acres and acres of open space for thousands of bunk beds — and there were also miles and miles of johns, urinals, sinks and showers along the entire outer wall. That first contingent of trainees occupied only a small part of that gargantuan building.

In the years since the war, I've heard many wild stories about how rough boot camp was, many more stories than I've heard about how tough combat was. You've heard them too: Mean and unreasonable drill seargeants, 25-mile forced marches with full packs, simulated night combat training exercises, etc. With one exception, my boot training was a snap — the cold and the boredom notwithstanding. We didn't have any seasoned basic training instructors; what we did have was a bunch of old-time chief petty officers who had been hurriedly recalled from retirement to make seaworthy sailors out of us in only six weeks' time. (The normal 12 weeks had been cut in half to meet the demands for personnel on new construction and to fill billets that had been "paper Navy" until Pearl Harbor was bombed.)

Before the end of the first week, word came that our boot training would be reduced to four weeks. By the end of the third week, we had been vaccinated and inoculated (how many times?), been exposed to some close-order drill, carefully schooled on the contents of the *Bluejackets' Manual,* and had been assigned a multitude of "busy" things to help occupy the time. Instead of six weeks, we had three weeks of training and were ". . . prepared to go out and win the war, Sir!" They didn't tell us why we were certified as combat-ready so quickly, of course, but a couple of things were obvious: The blizzard that hit the midwest about the first of the year never let up; the nights were all below zero and the daytime highs were all below freezing, so we never got to go outside. I never had seen so much ice and snow for so long a time. Too, the old chiefs who were training us had never had that kind of duty (or even been schooled in it), so they flat didn't know what to do or how to do it. There were only a few attempts at close-order drill (pretty pitiful), and the trainers and the trainees were so bad that each avoided the other whenever possible.

A couple of things do stand out in my mind about boot camp. The first taught me never to volunteer for anything. The first week of our training at the Pier was spent "policing the area"—which means cleaning it up. We scrubbed floors (they made us call them "decks"), cleaned windows and walls (portholes and bulkheads), sanitized the johns (heads, that is), and all those other important things that enable one to become an integral part of the fighting force on a wartime naval vessel. By the end of that first week, we were all pretty discouraged.

I thought I had found a way to avoid all this menial mopping and scrubbing johns and stuff when, at muster one morning ("muster" is Navy for "roll call"), the chief asked for volunteers: He said that he needed six men who could type or ride a motorcycle. I thought I could type even though I had flunked typing in high school (but 18 words per minute wasn't too bad) and I could ride a motorcycle. I had ridden on the back of one a few times and had watched the driver operate it—nothing to it. Besides, the chief said "ride" not "drive." Anyway, hands went up all over the place, probably 90 percent of the company. I could hardly believe my good fortune when I was one of the six trainees chosen. I was going to ask for a typing job. Company clerk. I would be there at my trusty typewriter in the cubicle that served as headquarters for the training company. For the rest of boot training, no more watches to stand and no more KP to draw. This is the way I thought I could best serve the Navy; I wanted something more than just a job ... and I thought I had it.

The chief marched us lucky volunteers away to our new assignment. We joined men from other training companies who were likewise as fortunate as we ourselves. We ended up in the armory, unpacking 30.06-caliber rifles that had been stored in cosmoline since the end of World War I. We worked our buns off, all 40 of us, eight hours a day for eight straight days. Rather, *they* worked eight days; I worked only three, and for a very legitimate reason! I was glad because this was my first experience with cosmoline. It adheres to whatever it comes in contact with; it takes gasoline or turpentine to get it off your skin but nothing can wash it out of your clothing. That experience was one of the worst three days I spent in the war. I was wearing a pair of those cosmoline-stained dungarees when we went ashore halfway around the world just a few months later.

*   *   *

The reason I spent only three days in the cosmoline was my feet. My shoes were such a poor fit that the longer I wore them, the bigger the blisters got. The second day on the rifle-cleaning detail, I went on sick call right after morning chow. The corpsman took one look at my blisters and called the doctor. My feet were a mess; big water blisters on both sides of both feet, one big one at the little toe of one foot and one huge one on the ball of the other. Both feet were pretty much covered with blisters. The doctor stuck needles in two of the biggest to drain them, swabbed both feet from the ankle down in Merthiolate, then covered both in bandages.

"Stay off your feet for a couple of days. Don't wear shoes or socks unless you have to."

The corpsman later told me that the doctor hadn't been in the Navy as long as I had been in, that he had reported for active duty on January 1st. No wonder he didn't know to give me a "light-duty" slip.

Sure, Doc. Whatever you say, sir.

Back to the armory and cosmoline.

I went back to Sick Bay late the next afternoon. My socks were bloody when the shoes came off. The corpsman took a pair of scissors and cut the socks off, then called the doctor again. One look and they wheeled me to the treatment room and spent one helluva long time opening up all the blisters and treating the raw, bloody places, which now covered most of the sides of both feet. I even had a blister on the top of one foot. After they were through, I was put to bed in sick bay and spent three nights and two whole days there. When I was released and sent back to duty, I had a chit from the doc requesting light duty for the next two weeks! I got my desk job after all.

Early the following Tuesday morning, the company clerk got a telephone call from the Supply Office, Great Lakes, ordering me to report to the supply officer. A car was en route and would pick me up in an hour.

"What the hell have you done, Kennedy?"

"I don't know, sir."

The civilian driver that picked me up didn't know either.

"All I know is I gotta take you back to the Supply CO's office."

It was a pleasant ride, even in traffic and bad weather. For some reason unknown to me, the driver insisted I sit in the back seat. It was a great ride. No admiral ever felt more important than I did that morning, leaning back in that deep seat with my legs crossed, reading the morning paper.

The supply officer was a commander. Annapolis man; you can't miss the ring. He had a pleasant look. I knew he was going to ask me something about shoes.

"Sailor, let's take a look at those feet."

I was about to get self-conscious about everybody staring at my lower extremities. It was obvious that he had had a call from the doc at Navy Pier. The upshot of the conversation (mostly his) was that I had to have shoes that fit and the Navy didn't know where to get them. He gave me a list of stores that one of his clerks had called, stores that carried "unusual sizes," and a Navy purchase order. The same civilian driver was told to take me to the stores listed – and any other stores until I had "a good pair of black shoes that fit and would meet Navy regulations."

It was noon when we got to the Loop, so the driver suggested we "get a bite to eat." He knew a little place where the "food is good and it don't cost too much." Quite a place. Small with the far end being a wall-to-wall bar. Maybe 12 to 14 tables with red and white checkered oilcloth covers. Sawdust on the floor; I had never seen that before – and the food was good; bratwurst and sauerkraut. He had a beer; I had a Coke – and the total bill for two was a little over two dollars. His treat but he did let me leave the tip, a dime and two nickels.

We did find shoes that fit but they were brown and/or sport shoes.

"We just don't get any calls for plain black shoes your size."

About four that afternoon, we hit pay dirt, almost-plain black shoes, size 13AAA. With a pair of Dr. Scholl's Odor-Eater insoles and an extra pair of socks, they fit just fine. When I signed the purchase order I thought the salesman had made a mistake: $16 for one pair of shoes! My last shoes, purchased just three months before, had cost $7 – the most that I had ever paid for one pair of shoes. I guess being handcrafted in England made the difference.

*   *   *

The other memory is an unusual experience on my first and only guard duty in boot camp. I was briefed by the watch petty officer that one of the trainees in our company was a bed-wetter. On my first 12-to-4 watch (guard duty), I had orders to wake this guy up every hour on the hour – all night – and escort him to the urinal and stand there with him until I saw him pass water. What happened was that this poor guy (who was also about 18 years old) was so homesick that he was ready to do almost anything, short of desertion, to get back home. He had heard somewhere in a scuttlebutt session that chronic bed-wetters got medical discharges and were sent home. So one night during our first weeks of training he began wetting the bed. I don't know if it is true or not, but we were told that he was seen the morning before lying on his side, penis in hand, soaking his bed. It was neater that way, I suppose; his bed was wet but he didn't have the unpleasantness of having to lie in it. The sailor turned himself in at sick bay as a bed-wetter. The doctor talked to him a while, took blood and urine samples and sent him back to duty with a couple of bottles of pills. Apparently the doc didn't believe the chronic bedwetting story, so he passed the word to our CO that this man was a gold-brick and that his bladder was to be emptied every hour each night until he was "cured" of his affliction. I had the mid-watch the second night of this guy's every-hour-to-the-john. And it was tough. The poor guy was exhausted from lack of sleep. His bladder was so empty that he was actually dehydrated and his stomach muscles were extremely sore from straining to help his bladder. He begged me to leave him alone, nearly cried. Nevertheless, I still had to drag him to the urinal and stand there with him until water was passed — even a drop would suffice. The night I had him, we had to stand there almost half an hour a couple of times. The third night we heard that he never even left the urinal.

The doctor knew best. Another medical breakthrough. After three full nights of an empty bladder, this poor guy never again suffered from this affliction! I saw him a couple of years later in New Caledonia and kidded him about the "problem" in boot camp. He grinned and told me that the cure was lasting, that he hadn't wet the bed since. His buddies told me that he was a good guy. And he did look sharp in his Class A green uniform; he was a combat medic attached to the First Marine Division. (Before he was assigned to a Marine unit, he had to undergo 12 weeks of Marine boot camp at Camp LeJeune, North Carolina, *after* he finished the 12-week medic school.)

*   *   *

In boot camp, they test everyone to see what he is best suited to do in the Navy, then assign him to a school to learn to do something else. I remember one guy in particular. Old guy, about 25. He had just received his law degree and had passed the bar exam a couple of months before the war started. He applied for a commission in the Judge Advocate General's office, but he was turned down because he flunked the eye test, so he enlisted. Did the guy get sent to the legal department? No, he was sent to cooks and bakers school. One of the guys I enlisted with was an exception. Lyonel loved to work on motors, any kind of motor, and he was good at it. He was sent to an aircraft mechanics school where he came out first in his class; he was then sent to duty on an aircraft carrier. One of the better examples of personnel utilization and management.

*　　*　　*

After our so-called boot training was over, most of us got overnight liberty before we left Chicago. The four weeks we had been confined (one at Great Lakes and three at Navy Pier) seemed more like a year. Three of us joined together for a great night on the town. Scuttlebutt had it that the Palmer House was now a Servicemen's Center. Perhaps this was before the days of the USO, I just don't remember, but I do remember the Palmer House; it had been one of the most elegant hotels in the midwest, maybe even the whole country, for a decade or so—and it was still the last word in elegance. Just about everything was free to anyone in uniform. For GIs, there was a reasonable, modest charge for food ordered in the dining room but it was a price we apprentice seamen could afford. Our pay at that time was $21 per month; we were paid $11 on the fifth and $10 on the twentieth less the withholding for our GI insurance premium and a buck or so to pay for the *Bluejackets Manual*. Our "take-home" was about $6 per payday.

*　　*　　*

The Palmer House was a dream come true. Elegant. There were two big-name bands playing in the clubs. One was Woody Herman and the other, I think, was one of the Dorsey brothers. We wandered in and out of both before going to the dining room for dinner. Wow, I had never seen so many spoons and forks at one plate. There was an older guy at the next table who looked comfortable with the way he was eating, so I watched him and picked up the system pretty quick: Small round spoon for the soup, small fork for the salad, etc. I didn't have to watch anybody to know how to attack the 20-ounce Kansas City strip sirloin steak—and I ate it all. The desserts were almost too pretty to eat. After dinner, we went back to one of the clubs and danced until after midnight. Lots of people there, all well-dressed; some of the women were in long evening dresses and men in tuxedos — and some of them had daughters with them, young daughters. There were very few uniforms in the club that night, so our sailor suits attracted a little attention. (Mine, especially; a small manufacturer's label was still sewn on my dress-blue jumper. A bellhop removed it for me.) Some of the daughters were pretty and some were downright good looking, but how do you go about picking up a gal when she's with her parents? New experience. I'll tell you how it's done: It's done very, very carefully. The fact that we were eyeing the young gals was pretty obvious — especially to their fathers. When I made a point of looking at one and she made a point of looking back, I suddenly realized her father was looking back too. It was then that I knew that I had to make my move: I immediately rose from my chair and went directly to their table and said to the girl's father, "Sir, may I dance with your daughter?"

"How do you know she wants to dance with you?"

She did, thank goodness, so I was spared that kind of embarrassment. We danced several times and I soon joined them at their table. Don't know what happened to the other guys, but the table was soon empty. They said later that they "got organized" and apparently had as good a time as I did. I didn't believe all of the yarns they spun, but they sure sounded good. My evening, compared to theirs, was mild. Why do most sailors feel like they have to tell everybody how they got laid ever time they go on liberty? (Maybe I always went to the wrong places.)

I really surprised myself that night. I walked from my table to the girl's father's table without stumbling over my feet and I spoke to the father without stuttering, spitting, or making an ass of myself. I was so suave I could hardly believe that this was me!

When we went on liberty that afternoon, I had a five-dollar bill and change in my pocket; when we got back to Navy Pier the next afternoon, I had about two dollars left. I had spent two bucks and a quarter on dinner and four bits for breakfast (plus tips). That's the way it was early in the war; when you were young and in uniform, most people didn't give you a chance to put your hand in your pocket. That night I didn't have to sleep with 180 other guys; I had my own private room and bath. What a way to go!

*   *   *

In just about any military outfit, there is always one guy who is an excellent storyteller. My Chicago liberty was with a storyteller named Leonard, a guy from Salt Lake City, maybe 21 or 22 years old, and another about my age, Henry, a cowhand from Muleshoe, Texas. Len was a gregarious person with a marvelous personality, the kind of guy you know who's going to "get some action" when he goes on liberty and you hope you can go with him so that maybe some of it will spill over on you. Hank was not that kind of person. He was quiet, too quiet most of the time, so much so that a lot of people who didn't know him very well thought maybe he wasn't very bright. Boy, were they wrong! Hank and I stayed together a long time, even through combat, and became friends, not real good friends, but friends who could and did trust each other. He was the kind of guy I looked for when the going got tough. I didn't know how three such different personalities came to go on liberty together, but off we went—and we all had a great time. After our "Palmer House liberty," Len told this story about Hank:

"We went to this really classy restaurant in the Palmer House, starched linen, bone china, lots of knives, forks, and spoons, waiters in tuxedos, *everything*. This big, white-headed waiter comes to our table to take our order and tells us all this stuff they didn't have room to print on the menu.

'Gentlemen, I recommend the chicken soup, it's a specialty of the house.'

"Me and Kennedy here, we ordered the soup, but not Hank.

'I don't like chicken soup,' Hank said.

'This is a chef's specialty, sir. I hope you won't be sorry,' returned the waiter.

'I still don't want no chicken soup,' Hank insisted.

'Very well, Sir.'

"We followed the waiter's suggestions for the rest of the meal—and we were not disappointed. Delicious.

"We lucked out on rooms. They weren't booked too heavy, so we each had a room all to ourselves. What we didn't know was that the room Hank got had been rented to an old guy that had lived there in the hotel for several years. He had a stomach problem of some kind and had to have an enema every day, so he hired a nurse who stopped by the hotel every day after she got off duty at the hospital, gave him an enema, then went on home.

"Well, the old guy died the morning of the day we checked in and the hotel clerk gave Hank the dead guy's room. Problem was, nobody told the nurse that the old guy had died, so she came to the hotel after the late shift that night and went to *Hank's* room. Hank was asleep and facing the wall when she came in. Thinking it was her patient and not wanting to disturb him any more than she had to, she didn't turn on the light in the room, but went quietly to the bathroom, prepared the enema, went back to the bed and pulled the covers back and stuck the hose up ole Hank's gazoo, then left.

"Next day, Hank's pa called him from Muleshoe and asked him how he was gettin' on in the Navy.

'Great,' Hank said, 'couldn't be better—and we went on our first liberty day before yesterday, to a place in Chicago called the Palmer House. The food there was great; I ate stuff there I didn't even know what it was. One thing, though, if you ever come to Chicago and go there and they try to get you to order the chicken soup, you gotta order it; if you don't, they may do to you what they did to me: they'll wait 'til you're asleep then come to your room and shove it up your ass.'"

Len told the story so well in the first person that there were a few who believed what he told about poor ol' Hank—and I was never sure about Len, whether or not he was trying to pull my leg.

*   *   *

After boot camp was officially over, we were all shipped back to the Receiving Station at Great Lakes where some of the guys got orders to proceed immediately to duty aboard ship or to naval installations somewhere around the world—and some of us were picked to go to specialized schools of some kind.

Why was I picked to go to aviation radio school? Perhaps there were quotas to fill. Must have been. I had no aptitude in that direction and had no desire to go to a technical school or any kind of school for that matter. I wanted to be a sailor on a ship, maybe a gunner's mate or a quartermaster. Actually, I didn't want to go to *any* school; I had been going to school all my life. All I wanted to do was get in the war as quickly as possible before it was all over. Imagine the embarrassment of being in military service and not getting to see combat. I wrote a formal Navy-type letter, thanked them for their confidence in me, and requested sea duty instead—on a fighting ship of course. Three days later, my orders came through: "Report to the Commanding Officer, Naval Aviation Radio School, NAS, Alameda, California."

The Training Process

There was one appealing thing about getting those orders that kept my big mouth shut: I was given a 30-day "delay en route," and a train ticket with Pullman accommodations from Chicago to Oakland, plus $5 a day while on the train. I was routed through Big Springs, Texas, 90 miles from home. Couldn't get all the way home because that particular rail line didn't go through Lubbock. The train was scheduled to arrive in Big Springs at 6 A.M. on a Wednesday, so I felt pretty sure I could hitch a ride and be home in time for breakfast.

One who hasn't gone first class on a Pullman doesn't know what luxury is. The food and service were excellent, and the dining car was a new experience. The service in the diner, the club car and the sleeper was "southern-style gracious," served by big black men who had mostly white hair; most of them had worked for the railroad all their lives in one capacity or another. And they always smiled big smiles that displayed two tiers of almost-perfect gleaming white teeth. Pullman porters and waiters made a good trip better, at least they did for me. And to this day, I've never seen a Pullman porter or waiter who was not pleasant and cheerful.

I traveled with what I considered an air of self-confidence. This was not my first train trip so I did know how to conduct myself. I had gone to Dallas on the train in 1939 when Lubbock High School played for the state football championship. (And I was a part of the team effort that gave our school and city the only state football championship it has ever had. I was one of the six cheerleaders.) I had also made a bus trip to Fort Worth when we played Northside High a year earlier. That was pretty much the extent of my travel on public conveyances but by no means the end of my travels — the most memorable being the time that Chuck Hawkins and I ran away from home in the summer of 1938. We were going to Burbank, California, to get jobs building airplanes.

We planned the trip carefully; we went to the freight office twice to check out trains, numbers, destinations, and times. When the time finally came, we knew exactly where to go and which train to board. We didn't know time schedules, but figured an empty freight would go straight through, so we figured we would be ready to apply for a job not later than three days from date of departure.

The airplane companies were paying the unheard of wage of $3 an hour. (Elsewhere in the United States, the hourly wage for unskilled labor was 50 cents.) It never occurred to either of us that we might not get a job the day we stepped off the freight train. Anyway, our runaway (or was it a defection?) was carefully planned; we sneaked away from home one night just before midnight, hopped an empty freight train, and were headed for California. We thought. The railroad detective who found us in that empty car appeared to be a stroke of good luck. Real nice man. He told us we were on the wrong car and then he even helped us find the right one. We told him our names when he asked, which turned out to have been the right thing to do. We thought he was being so helpful because he was the father of one of our classmates and because he and my father had known each other for years.

We were to discover later that this "friend of the family" purposely put us on a car that was being sidetracked at Muleshoe, Texas — about 60 miles west of Lubbock. Not only that, he also called my father that night and told him what he had done — then my dad called Chuck's dad. Looking back, can't say that I blame my dad for not coming down to the freight yard to get us; under the circumstances, I would probably have done the same. Both families knew we were gone before we even got out of the rail yard, but they stayed put and we left on the train as planned.

We enjoyed the ride in that empty car for the two hours before it stopped to switch cars. We didn't think anything was wrong until we had been sitting there the better part of an hour and we couldn't hear any more activity in the rail yard. By the time we realized that our car had been switched and sidetracked, it was too late to do anything about it; there was not another train in the yard, so we spent the rest of the night in that empty car.

We were on the highway early the next morning, hitchhiking to our fortune in California. We got a couple of pretty good rides, then a short one in the late afternoon that took us as far as the middle of nowhere in New Mexico — and I mean *nowhere*. The rancher who gave us the ride didn't tell us that there was nothing but a gate where he would be turning off for his place. We stood there on that lonesome highway until it was almost dark, thumbing every car — but they all passed us by. There we were, alone in the middle of the prairie — and we were cold, almost broke, and very hungry when a truck headed back toward Texas stopped and offered us a ride. We took it. He dropped us off at Klines Corner, New Mexico, where there was nothing but a couple of gas stations, a house and a cafe. After spending the night in an old abandoned car nearby, we mooched breakfast at the cafe, even tried to wash dishes to pay for the meal, then made the decision to go back home before we starved to death. We had been gone just over two days.

We hit the highway, US Route 66, about seven that morning and were still standing there at eleven, our thumbs pointing east. There was a pretty good flow of traffic, enough that we should have gotten a ride, but no one would stop. We finally decided that the drivers of the cars were wary of *two* young male hitchhikers, that we might do them in and steal their car. The only way to get a ride, we decided, was to split up. We tossed a bottle cap (didn't have a coin) to see who would stay put and who would walk a quarter of a mile up the highway. I lost, so I walked to my new spot. We knew that Chuck would get a ride first, and when he did he was supposed to say to the driver, "That's my cousin there. Can you give him a ride too?"

Lo and behold, the very next vehicle stopped, but he didn't stop for Chuck; he stopped for *me!*

"Where ya goin', kid?"

"Lubbock."

"I'm goin' to Amarillo. Get in, I'll let you off at Tucumcari or you can go on with me."

I didn't get off at Tucumcari, I rode on in to Amarillo, and once there made a beeline to my Aunt Georgie's house. She wasn't surprised to see me, even though she didn't know I was coming. When she heard what I had done, there were no recriminations but she told me I was going to get it when I got home. She said I looked hungry, so she fried up a batch of ham and eggs (six, all told, sunny side up) and fed me, then took me to the bus station and bought me a ticket home. She said I was going to catch it at home — and I did.

Chuck got two rides that got him to Lubbock and when he got home, he caught it too. Both sets of parents had gotten together and decided that we "were a bad influence on each other" and that we were to discontinue our friendship. We didn't, of course, and I suppose we should have been grateful for the edict because it made us even closer friends.

(There is much more to this story!)

*   *   *

Meanwhile, back on the Pullman...

I read, napped, and enjoyed the scenery as the train rolled southwest, headed for Texas. At dinner that night (we called the evening meal "supper" back home) the headwaiter seated me at table. In the dining car, no one had a table all to himself; all seats had to be filled. Shortly after I was seated, I was joined by an elderly gentleman and a young couple about 25, all en route to the west coast. It was a good meal and enjoyable; we talked about things in general. The old gentleman didn't have much to say and excused himself soon after he finished his coffee and dessert, but the young couple stayed on and we talked about a lot of things — except the war and why they were going to the coast. The way they talked, they sounded like they were "with the government," or had something, somehow, to do with the war. The headwaiter finally asked us to "excuse ourselves" so that others waiting for dinner could be seated. (My check was for $3.20, including tip — the most I had ever paid for one meal.)

There was a young couple in the club car playing cards when I came in. They invited me over for a drink, I suppose, because I was the only person on the train in uniform. Instead of the beer I ordered, the stewart brought me an orange soda after he checked my ID and saw that I was barely 19 years old. The woman, her husband, and I exchanged introductions and idle chatter. When we had about run out of anything to say, she asked if I wanted to play a little gin rummy. She was good; sure am glad we were not playing for money. I don't remember their names, but he was big and muscular (like a defensive tackle) and she was slim and a very good-looking woman, well filled out in all the places that were supposed to be well filled. Since I had a 5:30 A.M. wake-up, I told my friends good night about 9:00 and headed for my Pullman. I had an upper, three berths from the end of the car.

When my wake-up came, I pulled on my pants, grabbed my ditty bag (the Navy's version of a Dopp kit; it was a canvas bag with a drawstring of thin rope and was about the size of a basketball), and headed for the men's lavatory. I shaved, brushed my teeth, and slicked up as best I could without a shower and headed back to my sleeper, three berths from the end of the car. Problem was, I went to the third upper at *the wrong end of the car!* Not realizing the mistake, I pulled back the curtains, tossed my ditty bag inside, and lifted myself up and sat on the edge of the berth. I reached back for

my bag—and *froze*. There was a woman asleep in that berth, lying
on her left side with her nightgown pulled up around her waist—and
my hand was *not* resting on my ditty bag; it was resting right smack
on her bare bottom!! It was the woman I played gin rummy with in
the club car. Thank heaven she was a sound sleeper; she didn't
move—and neither did I. The instant my hand touched that
woman's fanny, I thought of a dozen things, all bad: If she awakens,
she'll scream "RAPE" and I'll spend the next 20 years in the naval
prison at Portsmouth if her husband doesn't beat me to death first,
or I'll get kicked out of the Navy and miss the war—and all kinds
of things like that. What I did, finally, was to ease my hand off her
bare rear, grab my ditty bag, jump down to the aisle and run like
hell back to the men's lavatory. Apparently she slept through it.
When there was no outcry, I walked back to *my* berth, finished
dressing, and got off the train as scheduled, unscathed. (Wonder
what she thought when she awakened the next morning and found
her sleeper curtains wide open? And I also wonder how in the world
that ditty bag missed hitting her right on the tail when I threw it
through that open curtain?)

*   *   *

My 30 days at home were great—mostly social and civic and I
was the center of attention, being one of the first of the hometown
enlistees to come home in uniform; I had been in the Navy less than
two months. There were many parties and a lot of night life. Before
the leave was over, even though I had a great time, I was ready to
get on with my new life in the Navy. No sailor ever had less boot
training than I did but enough rubbed off that made me feel like a
sailor at least. The term "on the job training" hadn't yet been coined,
but those of us who had been rushed through training knew that
what we lacked in training would be gained in the experience process—and that is exactly what happened, but not the way we expected it to happen. What the American forces, worldwide, lacked
in experience and materiel was compensated for with guts and imagination. Examples of this ingenuity will show, I think, in some of
the things that happened during the war as I was involved in it.

*   *   *

After the month at home, I went back to Big Springs and
caught the train to California. It was an eventful trip but not anything like the Chicago–Big Spring leg; it seemed like everybody was

on their way to California. I was fortunate enough to get a roomy seat next to an older lady who didn't speak English very well, so I read and napped a good deal, resting up from the rigors of the night life back in Lubbock, Texas. And I made darn sure I knew where *my* sleeper was in relation to the men's lavatory. Couldn't take a chance on another attempted rape or anything like that.

When the train pulled into the station in Oakland on February 28, 1942, I was apprehensive because I didn't know where Alameda was nor did I know how to get there. I was relieved the minute I walked out of the main entrance of the depot (except that they call them "terminals" in California). There were military vehicles parked and standing all over the place. I asked a shore patrolman how to get to NAS, Alameda. He pointed to a bus parked at the curb and said, "Take that one." When we left a few minutes later, it was full; all aboard were going to the Aviation Radio School there.

It was a huge, beautiful military installation. It was a Naval Air Station but it appeared that there were no fighting nor patrol squadron operations; it was a total training facility, both ground and air. The barracks were enormous, spotlessly clean, and freshly painted. Just about everyone on that bus reported in to the Officer of the Day who called for the Chief Master-at-Arms, a burly old chief who (we learned later) had been in the Navy nearly 30 years! He was old enough to be my grandfather. Nice old guy. He wasn't like any other chief in the Navy; he was low-key and patient, but there was an undercurrent of authority that made you know you'd be in trouble if you ran afoul. He gave us a little lecture, I suppose you'd call it, about the base and where everything was, then assigned us to sleeping quarters.

The section I was assigned to housed about 200 men, but the double-deck bunks and lockers were arranged in "bays" in such a way that took away from the vastness of the place. I was quite pleased with my temporary new home. But it wasn't to be home for very long.

The barracks were almost full, but classes were not to begin for another two weeks; the spare time, however, was not to be spent in idleness. We had orientation lectures, sex hygiene lectures, lecture on the Articles of War, and more lectures on sex hygiene (the Navy was overly concerned with sex and venereal disease). We heard so much about sex in that two-week period we were beginning to think that they thought we were all sex maniacs and that all the girls in the Bay area had communicable diseases. It's amazing what good leadership can do without an agenda: Show another sex film. It wasn't really that bad, but it seemed so at the time. It was "busy time" with films and lectures to keep us occupied; a lot of the guys griped about "this is the same kind of stuff we just had in boot camp." Not me. This was a learning experience I missed in boot camp and needed very badly.

When I enlisted, the base pay for an apprentice seaman was not very much, only $21 a month — less deductions. After shaving gear, toothpaste, and cigarettes, there wasn't a lot of money left over. There was not much point in going on liberty with no money and no place to go. It was early in the war, so early that the USO was still pretty much in the planning stage. The only liberty I pulled for the few weeks I was stationed at NAS Alameda was on Sunday mornings. Old habits die hard; war or not, Sunday mornings were still church mornings. I went to the Base Chapel only once. It was a nondenominational service, nothing at all like I was accustomed to in the Methodist church.

Even though I was a little uncomfortable doing it, I did go to the chaplain and ask his advice: I didn't like the military protestant service. Fortunately for me, he was a Methodist. He told me that near the center of Oakland, there was a nice big place called "Seamen's Center" or "Servicemen's Center" — I don't remember which. If I got to the Center before 10 A.M., there were always people there with cars to take servicemen to church — and after church they usually took you home with them for a nice Sunday dinner. Off I went. At the Center, there were placards placed around the room with the various denomination names. All I had to do was find "Methodist" and stand there by the sign. It wasn't long before a nice looking older gentleman came up and introduced himself, then took me out to the car to meet his wife. We went immediately to the church.

I liked the church very much. Since we arrived a little early, I was shown through the series of buildings that housed the some 1,000 members. Even though it was bigger, it was very much like the church back home — and so was the order of service except that the sermons were shorter. (Brother Robinson sure liked to preach.) After church the host family took me to their home for the same kind of Sunday dinner that just about everybody in the rural southwest has — fried chicken, mashed potatoes, cream gravy, Parker House rolls, and all the trimmings. It was a good day for a lonesome kid who was a long way from home. I went to church there every Sunday for the few weeks I was at NAS and was the guest of a new family each week. This turned out to be the welcome part of a weaning process that was to take me from a high school in west Texas to a chain of islands halfway around the world that most people had never heard of.

*   *   *

After four months as an apprentice seaman, promotion to seaman second class was automatic (if you hadn't screwed up) and the pay jumped from $21 to an astronomical $36 per month. First-class seaman put you in the big money bracket: $68 per month, before deductions. Since I was still an apprentice seaman, I was broke all the time. Movies on the base were free, but I needed a project, a goal to work toward. It took a while to find one, but I chose a beauty: Algebra. I had brought a math textbook with me when I left home, the one I needed to prepare for the exam that I knew I had to take someday. With a little help from a few of the guys who knew math, I began a systematic course of study, having no idea that I would take an algebra exam in less than a month.

One of the trainees in the radio school was a school teacher from Baird, Texas. When I learned that he taught math in the high school there, I talked to him about my problem with algebra and asked if he would help. He would — and he did. He not only tutored me but he called my principal at Lubbock High and told him of my wish to finish up that last half credit in algebra so that I could graduate. He not only tutored me, he administered the exam sent from the school! I'll never forget the relief I felt when I sat down to take it, the simplest algebra exam anyone had ever been given. I guess the school principal or the math department or somebody back there thought I wasn't going to make it back. I passed it in a breeze. The letter acknowledging my achievement came from the principal and congratulated me warmly; he affirmed that I was now a graduate of Lubbock High School and that the diploma would be awarded, in absentia, at some later date. I felt great! Before I got home after my part in the war, I was lucky that it hadn't been awarded posthumously.

The radio school wasn't easy. I was doomed from the beginning because not only did I not want to be there in the first place, I had no desire to repair or operate a radio that didn't play music. All I wanted to do was shoot a gun. I wrote a letter to the base commander and asked for a transfer to sea duty; I said that I wanted to be on a "fighting ship." Naval Personnel responded quickly — and before the first of May, 1942, I had orders to the Naval Net Depot, Tiburon, California. Nobody I talked to seemed to know anything about nets in the Navy, but they did know where Tiburon was; it was across the bay from San Francisco, located on the water exactly one mile from the main entrance to San Quentin State Penitentiary. (Another interesting point: it was very close to Alcatraz. When the liberty boat took us to and from San Francisco, prisoners, sailors, and guards all waved to each other.)

The Slab

I'll never forget the day of my transfer. About a half-dozen of us had orders to the same place, so we boarded a Navy bus and were taken to the Port of San Francisco. At dock-side, the bus stopped at the sleekest, most shipshape new destroyer escort I have ever seen; it appeared to be newly commissioned, and it was all mine — I thought! Duty would be great on this sleek warship. We shouldered our sea bags (there were six of us, all from the radio school) and went aboard, only to be told by the Officer of the Deck to keep moving to the other side of the ship. There, tied up alongside the destroyer escort, was the raunchiest old bucket of bolts I have ever seen; it was a net tender whose home port was the Naval Net Depot at Tiburon. The duties of the crew of seven on that tender was to lay and tend antisubmarine nets and to lay torpedo baffle around ships anchored or moored in positions where they were exposed to enemy submarine action.

My orders, however, were not to the tender, but to the depot to which the tender was attached. Once off the ship and on the pier, I looked at my new duty station and almost got sick to my stomach. This sure as hell didn't look like any kind of naval station that I had ever heard of. Here was this tired old ex-excursion boat tied up to a big old concrete pier piled high on one side with buoys, huge spools of wire, all kinds of crates, and a couple of fork lifts. Beyond the boat were several warehouse-type buildings, and at the far end an outside work area called the Slab. This place looked like work — and it was! Up until the day we left the place, it remained the same rough-and-tumble place of toil — but the place seemed to grow on the sailors stationed there and a kind of pride of accomplishment grew on us as our sweat added to the quality of nets and baffle we turned out. None of us actually liked the place, but we were proud of the job that was accomplished.

Conditions on base got a little better as we became a part of what was going on there — but not much. The primary duty of the net depot was to assemble (manufacture, actually) the nets that would be laid across harbors sheltering naval vessels. A net tender manned the "gate" that opened and closed to let friendly ships in and out.

The base itself, in reality, wasn't too bad; it was the duty that was rough and dirty. Personnel-wise, there must have been 500 officers and enlisted men stationed there. The enlisted men were billeted aboard the "Delta Queen," in her glory days an old rear paddlewheeler that used to be a tourist excursion boat up and down the Sacramento River. Even though she was pushing forty years of age, she still had some of her former elegance. The Navy had taken her over a few years before for office space and billets. The sailors at the Net Depot worked at "the Slab" — a piece of concrete about the size of a basketball court with six-inch spikes protruding in a diamond-like geometrical design. It was here that we would manhandle spools of half-inch mesh steel wire treated in a substance very much like cosmoline in some ways, but much thicker than axle grease and black as tar. That wire had to be interwoven between those spikes until there was a pattern of four-foot diamonds (or squares) about 25 feet deep and about 75 feet long. After the steel wire had been properly laid, we then went back to where the wires crossed and secured each piece firmly with a heavy clamp. It was back-breaking, filthy work. The grease covered our hands, arms, and clothing — and sometimes our faces. We could get the grease off our bodies with kerosene, but our pants, shirts, and shoes were shot. Since we paid for our own clothing in the Navy, we continued to wear the stiff, stinking blue work clothes and shoes until they literally fell off our bodies — which usually took two or three weeks.

After the nets were assembled on the slab, the really tough, dirty work took place: We had to hand-fold and tie them together in such a manner that they could be laid in place in the water by the tender after a single wire was cut. Assembling the torpedo baffle was not that bad. We had sections of quarter-inch aluminum hoops about 12 inches in diameter that interlocked and were in sections of about 25 feet by 50 feet. These were not coated and were made of a lightweight material, not aluminum but a light metal like it. These sections were to be attached, one to another, until they could be laid around a ship (perhaps 40 feet from its hull) so that a torpedo striking it would be cushioned and not explode. Japanese torpedoes exploded only on contact; if it missed the target, it would continue to run until it ran out of fuel, then sink. An American torpedo, on the other hand, was not only set to explode on contact but would explode after a certain number of revolutions if it missed the target.

Talk about rough duty, that was it! We worked all day — eight hours — on the Slab, then had to fall in for calisthenic exercises that ended with jogging uphill (about a 15 percent grade) out of the entrance to the base and on to the gates of San Quentin State Prison — a two-and-a-half-mile round trip. After that, we were free to clean off the grease and grime, shower, and go on liberty. I didn't make liberty for the first couple of months there because I was too tired and too broke. I was so tired that I usually cleaned some of the grease off, then lay down on the deck by my bunk and rested for half an hour hoping that I would gain enough strength to shower and clean up. Didn't have any money because I was still an apprentice seaman who had almost zero spendable income. There was nothing left after buying shaving gear, toothpaste, writing gear and stamps, and cigarettes. The month I was paid as a seaman second class, I took all that extra money — all 15 big dollars — and went to San Francisco on a liberty like no other sailor ever had, literally!

*   *   *

Some of the old-timers on the base and the liberty-hounds talked about the great times they had at a bar in San Francisco called "Pinocchio." Lots of good lookin' girls, civilians who wouldn't let a sailor pay for a drink, good combo, dancing, and all the things that would appeal to a lonely, homesick, somewhat disillusioned young sailor. And I sure did yearn for some feminine companionship!

I had the duty the weekend of payday, so I didn't get my liberty until Monday after chow — and I was ready: Shaved, showered, liberally doused with bay rum (which was the aftershave worn by all discerning gentlemen), and in freshly pressed, clean navy blue dress uniform. I caught the liberty boat for the Embarcadero in 'Frisco and took a bus to Pinocchio's. Got there early, before 8, so there was not much going on. I sat at the bar and sipped on a beer while the juke box played the favorite tunes of the day until the combo came on at nine. (Some bars would serve minor GIs on off-hours when the Shore Patrol was not likely to come around.) I sat and sipped very slowly on my beer because it was expensive, 35 cents per bottle plus tip. Wow! Expensive, but worth it.

Before I finished my Budweiser (they had never heard of Lone Star), people began straggling in. Among them were two girls, very good looking, who took a table close to the dance floor. I gave them what I thought was a suave look and much to my surprise, the better looking of the two winked at me! Not a big wink, but enough to let me know that she knew I was aware that she was there. Even though she did appear older, maybe 23 or 24, I sauntered over to the table like any old salt would do (rather, I imagined what they would do since I had never been on the make like that before) and asked her if she would like to dance. She would and she did. Boy, did she! The first dance, though, was done like we were being chaperoned at a church picnic; she wouldn't even dance cheek to cheek. And we could have, because she was nearly six feet tall. The next dance, after another beer, was closer, and by the third dance, she was grinding her hips into mine so hard I had to grind back to keep from falling backward. Suffice it to say, the young lady—whose name was Francie—did arouse me a little. Ha. While we were dancing, her friend left the table to join another group, so Francie and I had it alone. And the guys at the base were right—she insisted on paying for all the drinks and anything else we wanted, but I gallantly said no. It didn't matter right then because it was all on the tab, but I had mixed emotions; I was taught that the male always paid the way. After the third drink, when I knew my bankroll was getting close to pocket change, I made a feeble attempt to leave. Francie knew what was bothering me.

"Sweetie, don't worry about it. I work for a ship building company and all this goes on my expense account."

We danced a few more times, but not many because her contortions and the intimate things she whispered to me became more and more erotic and more explicit. To make a long story short, we decided to go to her place.

"For a nice quiet drink where we can relax. Besides, if the Shore Patrol comes around and checks your liberty card, you could be in trouble."

I couldn't believe this was happening to me; Lubbock, Texas, was never like this. Anyway, her car was in the parking lot, but before she started the engine, we did a little smoochin'—and then we did a little more—and then we got serious! In the process, my hands got out of control and I ended up playing with her legs, and then I began playing for higher stakes. Strange that she was so touchy about my not feeling anything above the waist. Things seemed to be going my way and I was pleased with whatever I was doing because this girl was eating it up! Then I made the final grab—and at first I did not believe what was happening, but there it was, there was no getting around it; I was dumbfounded: *Francie was not a girl at all!!*

She (it?) was a male, dressed and made up like no gal I had ever seen before. It took a minute before I finally flung the door open and jumped out of the car, mad as hell and frustrated beyond imagination — and saying, rather shouting, everything that came from my mixed-up emotions. All I heard as I cleared the parking lot was, "Don't be mad. Please don't be mad."

I went back to the ship and brushed my teeth and gargled 'til midnight.

I made the mistake of telling the guys about what happened — and I was sorry I did because they never let me forget it. You wouldn't believe the ribbing I got. I was glad when they quit calling me Romeo. Oh well, it did bring some humor into an otherwise tough and dreary tour of duty. And I learned something from it too: I added the word "transvestite" to my vocabulary. I'd never heard the word before, and that was my one and only hands-on experience with one.

*   *   *

Duty on the Slab was the pits; it was so bad that when we got KP or guard duty, it was like getting a day off. There were no desertions while I was there but a lot of guys went AWOL. When they came back, the sentence was always the same: Three to ten days in the brig on bread and water, depending on how long they had been gone. The mess cooks had to take the bread and water and give it to the prisoners, one meal per day. There was an unwritten rule in the galley: For the prisoners, if you could pour it, it was water; if it was solid enough to break, it was bread. Our prisoners always got plenty to eat, even if it was only one meal a day.

*   *   *

There was a guy at Tiburon named Stanley; everyone knew Stanley and everyone kept as far away from Stanley as possible. My bunk was maybe eight feet away from his until I was fortunate enough to move to quarters in another section of the ship. I was one of the fortunate ones.

Stanley was a Yankee, from "Noo Joisey" as he pronounced it, and people seemed to like him, from afar. He had no friends because no one wanted to be in his immediate proximity very long unless it was absolutely necessary, and all for a very good reason: Stanley didn't bathe or wash his clothing. Almost never.

Dungarees were our work clothing; they consisted of light blue chambray shirts, medium-blue heavy cotton trousers and white socks. After working all day at the Slab at hard labor, the first thing we did once back in quarters was to strip off and head for the showers — but not Stanley; he laid on his bunk until chow time and followed that same routine every day. While we showed up for muster every morning in freshly washed dungarees, he had on the same clothing that he had worn the day before — and the day before that, et cetera; his blue chambray shirt was mostly brown from dirty sweat, his trousers were caked with crud, and his once-white socks were a dark brownish color. We kidded him about not having to use a hanger for his clothes, that all he had to do was stand them in the corner when he took them off. He thought that was funny. Actually, he was a pretty nice guy and had a good sense of humor, but the good attributes ended right there; he was not only dirty but he stank to the high heaven. Never have I been exposed to a more offensive body odor.

We complained to the chief, who promised to "take action" and were surprised and pleased when Stanley showed up for muster the next morning in clean dungarees which he continued to wear for the next two weeks. I don't think he went so far as to take a shower. That body odor! It was so bad that it permeated the living area. When an old salt (career sailor) was transferred into the outfit, the first thing he did when he stepped through the door of the living quarters was to ask a question.

"What the fuck died in here and how long ago?"

This new sailor was a no nonsense kind of guy and, as it turned out, had the answer that paved the way to a new life of good hygiene for Walter Stanley.

Couple of days later he said, "I can't live with this shit any longer. We've gotta go with the sand and canvas tonight."

I didn't know what this meant and neither did anyone else. When I asked the chief, he pretended he didn't hear and walked off. Strange.

That night the new sailor (we called him Shanghai; he didn't seem to have any other name) came to our bunks and awakened four of us and led us to the shower. There he had laid out about a half-dozen pieces of canvas sail, cut into two-foot squares, and two buckets of sand. He had us strip down to our shorts, then led us back to Stanley's bunk. Stanley tried to fight when we began pulling him out of the bunk but Shanghai had such a tight stranglehold on his neck that I thought his eyes were going to pop out. Getting him to the shower was not the easy task we thought it would be. Without Shanghai, I think Stanley could have whipped us all.

Sand and canvas means a shower using sand as the cleaning agent and canvas as a wash cloth, using plenty of water. It took three of us to hold him down while the other two scrubbed; we took turns holding him down and scrubbing him. We scrubbed every inch of Stanley's body from the chin down, with emphasis on his underarms and private parts — and we scrubbed hard. We scrubbed until he screamed with pain, but no one from the sleeping quarters or from the Duty Office came forward to interfere with this time-honored Navy practice of helping someone to lead a clean life.

It was over in about 15 minutes. Stanley was panting, heaving, crying, and bleeding. Blood oozed from every pore of his body and there was a bloody imprint of his rear end on the bench in the shower where he sat after we finished. When it was over and we were going back to our bunks, Shanghai told Stanley that the first time was "just a warning," that he only got a once-over-lightly this time. The next time, he said, some real hard scrubbing goes on.

What happened that night was never discussed, even among those of us who were the perpetrators/participants, nor did Stanley ever say anything. He did go to Sick Bay that morning before reveille. He didn't volunteer any explanation to the corpsman nor was he asked for one. He was back in the Duty Office about mid-morning with a slip from the doctor requesting light duty for two weeks. He spent those two weeks in the ship's laundry, wearing only his skivvies.

Happy ending! After the scabbing sloughed off, Stanley was seen using the showers regularly, and he put on clean clothing every day. Even used deodorant.

Emergency Leave

I n early June of 1942, I received a bad news letter from home. It came as no surprise because my father, in his mid seventies, had not been very healthy for the last two or three years. Even though he went to work every day, he was a very sick man. He never admitted how sick he was and he continued to work right up to the week he died. This was what a man was supposed to do: go to work every day. He'd walk to the store to work for just an hour or so. Age, of course, had a lot to do with it. Pop was about 54 or 55 years old when I was born, so this put him up to 73 or 74.

The letter was from my sister; she told me that Pop had cancer of the stomach — that's all they knew. (When he died a year later, the autopsy showed cancer of the liver, pancreas, and spleen.)

The executive officer of the base was an old "mustang" — an enlisted man commissioned from the ranks. He was a crusty old bugger, about 60, who had been recalled from retirement. He was the kind of man who spoke in a growl, and everybody on the base was scared to death of him, so it was with bated breath, fear and trepidation, that I entered his office, letter in hand. He read it and growled as usual, but this particular growl was worth a 10-day emergency leave. With tears of joy, I thanked him, saluted sharply, and turned to leave. His parting compassionate words to me were, "And if you're one hour late gettin' back here, you're gonna spend the rest of this here goddam war in the brig. Unnerstand?"

"Yessir."

I left the base less than an hour later with my leave papers, a small hand-bag, and $4.25 in my pocket. I took exactly two days, hitchhiking day and night, to get to Lubbock. I had not written anyone that I was coming, but they were expecting me anyway. I had $1.20 in my pocket when I arrived.

Hitchhiking in those days was easy if you wore a uniform. Usually it was only a matter of minutes from the time one car let you out until another picked you up. Getting home this time was pretty much routine except for one incident. When I left the base in California, it was late afternoon, so I hitchhiked all night and all the next day. The following night, I had gotten as far as some little town in New Mexico — I don't remember the name. It was awfully late at night, but I walked to the edge of town and stood under a streetlight with my thumb pointed east. I was dead tired and almost asleep on my feet. There was hardly any traffic. A kid came riding down the road on his bicycle, stopped and started talking to me about the war. I'm sure that he could see that I was about out on my feet, so he said, "Why don't you come to my house and spend the night, then get an early start in the morning? I live in that house down there."

I walked to the house with him and waited on the porch while he went in to ask his mother. He finally came to the door and said, "Come on in."

He got a pillow and a blanket and told me I could sleep on the couch. It was a modest little four-room house. I could just imagine how angry his mother must have been and how frightened, alone in the house with a strange sailor, but I was too tired to leave. I awakened about 4 A.M., found an old envelope on the floor and wrote a brief "thank you" on the back of it and left it on the couch. I was a little kindness I have never forgotten.

I had six days at home. It was a memorable leave in more ways than one. I spent a lot of time with Pop. Sometimes conversation was awkward because we didn't have a lot to say to each other. But I was so very thankful for the feeling of love and understanding that existed between us. In that day and time, you didn't mention the word "cancer" to a cancer victim, nor did they dare mention it to you. We talked a little about the war and the weather, played dominoes sometimes, and at other times just sat in silence, very comfortable with each other's presence. That time alone with Pop is one of the sweet memories of my life. Even though he knew I was in the Solomon Islands, every morning until the day he died, he said, "Wipe the moisture off the windows, mother, so I can see Billie when he comes up the walk."

My mother didn't even tell me when he died, nor would she let anyone else. When I called home from the hospital at Mare Island when I got back from the war, I talked to her and then asked to speak with Pop. It was then that she told me he had been dead for months. She said she was afraid to write me at the time, and finally decided to wait until I got back so I could "handle it better." She was partially right about my being able to handle it. I couldn't handle not being told. She said she didn't tell me "while you were out there under the strain of combat."

How ironic. I saw and lived with death every day, death on both sides. It was the one thing I could handle well at that particular time in my life.

That leave to see Pop before he was so sick is one of those special things a young boy stuck back in a recess of his mind and pulls out to treasure on special occasions for the rest of his life. Mine and Pop's relationship was something special, an unspoken bond that didn't have words to describe it. And that's a good thing, I guess. It's not like an English sentence you have to diagram, or a math problem you have to solve. In the end, it sort of turned out to be something of a mystery that we shared and cherished. He did and I still do.

*   *   *

The commencement exercises were held the week I was home with Pop — and I looked forward to being a part of it, but the school told me I had been included with the midterm class so couldn't be included with the spring graduates. I intended to go to the exercises that night, even went to the high school, but didn't go into the auditorium. I sat on a bench in the park across the street until it was over. There was a reception in the gym afterward. I went in and stayed for a little while, then went home early. I realized, finally, that I didn't belong in that kind of world anymore, that my life had gone from one extreme to the other.

*   *   *

I gave myself two and a half days to get back to the base. I made it in two, hitchhiking straight through, day and night. It was the best leave a sailor ever had — and there was no "action" at all.

*   *   *

By June, 1942, things were tough all over. The Japanese had a stranglehold on the Pacific; the only thing that kept them from the west coast was the naval base at Pearl Harbor. Even though they had already sunk most of the Pacific fleet, we still had all our carriers and enough other big stuff to make our presence felt. Things weren't much better in Europe. The United States did not yet have the trained manpower to commit to the allied effort there, so they were sending hundreds of shiploads of supplies and war materiel to the allies in Europe and more to the Russians at Murmansk — most of which, it seemed, was sunk by the German U-boats in the north

Atlantic. Over a million men and women were in training camps all over the country by this time. (There would be over 11 million men and women in uniform by the end of the war.) Trained personnel were at a premium and all branches of the service were clamoring for qualified men to be trained as pilots; the need was so great that both Army and Navy lowered their requirements for flight training: Men aged 18 and over with a high school diploma were eligible to apply to the cadet corps. Previously, the requirement was age 21 and two years of college.

Navy Wings?

The revised requirements for Navy flight training were announced a couple of days before my emergency leave was up. As soon as I read about the possibility of getting in the program, I made a beeline to the Navy Recruiting Station at the Post Office Building in Lubbock, back to the same office where I had chosen the shorter line just a few short months ago.

"You can apply to the Naval Aviation Cadet Selection Board at the Embarcadero in San Francisco."

What luck! The liberty boat ran from Tiburon to the Embarcadero twice a day, so I could apply in person the minute I got back off leave. Hot dawg! This was one school that I wasn't going to mind at all. I daydreamed all the way back to base, all 1800 miles, about flight training and flying a Grumman Wildcat. What were my chances of making it to flight school?

When I finally got back to base, the only thing that kept me from going directly to the Selection Board was the hour; I got back at 9 P.M. — three hours before my leave was up. Three days later, I got early liberty and went in on the first boat, found the Naval Aviation Cadet Selection Board office and went in.

I approached the WAVE on duty at the reception desk and told her what I was there for. She gave me a sheaf of papers to read along with the application. It was long and detailed, so much so that it took nearly two hours to complete because it included the required information for a security check. The ensign to whom I returned it told me to come back the following Wednesday for the written exams. I was the first one there that Wednesday morning, but I had lots of company. There must have been 50 of us to take that three-hour exam. Except for the timed exams, I went over and over my answers. The same ensign took my papers when the last minute expired and told me that the results would be ready "in about 10 days. You will hear from us, one way or the other."

You can't imagine how heavily the time weighed as I waited for the letter or for orders. Precisely ten days later, I received a letter from the Board: *I passed!*

The letter from an admiral congratulated me and told me to report on a given date for the physical exam, and if I passed it, I would then appear for an interview with the members of the Selection Board "for a final determination." As I recall, the interview was scheduled for the first week in July. They sent me to the Naval Hospital on Mare Island for my physical. I was a little on the skinny side, but everything was A-OK!

At the appointed time and hour for my interview with the Selection Board, I was there precisely to the minute (Regular Navy, especially, like punctuality). The same ensign met me again; there had been a foul-up of some kind on the paperwork, he said. I was told that members of the military had a six-month waiting period from the date of application, something to do "within channels." When I told the ensign we expected to get shipped out almost any time, he told me that I should apply for a waiver and even showed me what kind of letter I had to submit, and told me it had to go through the "proper channels"—through my base commander, to the Naval District, to the Selection Board. I wrote the letter and personally handed it to the chief yeoman in the skipper's office.

"I'll get the skipper's signature on it and will have it on the way no later than tomorrow."

And then I waited—and waited.

Back at the Slab, things began to ease up. We had made about 50 sections of antisubmarine netting and enough torpedo baffle to go around every ship in the Pacific that was still afloat. We were so caught up, the brass thought it would be a good idea if we were given further training in maintenance, such as how to weld, how to use a cutting torch, how to operate a bulldozer and how to man small boats. Some of us even got some underwater training in tending the nets. Instead of the dirty drudgery of the Slab, the training we were now getting was actually pleasant, or at least a welcome relief. Something was up, but we knew not what. Meanwhile, I waited for word on my waiver, but it never came; at least, it didn't come before we got orders to ship out on July 18, 1942. The shipping out orders were read at the 5 P.M. muster; we were told to be ready at 1800 hours, 6 P.M. We had less than an hour to be ready to ship out. When we were ordered to "Fall Out," I was the first to get to the pay phone booth on the pier, so made a quick collect call home. "All I know is you can write me care of Cub One, Fleet Post Office, San Francisco."

Off to the War...

W
e were off to the war — we hoped. During all this training, combat areas were not even mentioned. From the
kind of duty we were trained to perform, we assumed
that the best we could hope for, as far as combat was concerned, was
a rear echelon support group where we would throw the antisubmarine net across a harbor to protect a shore station so our ships
could come in and anchor for unloading or for repairs. Wherever
we were going and whatever we would be doing was a welcome
relief. Tiburon was not exactly choice duty and we were sick of the
Slab. Even so, we were ready; all the other training procedures had
helped to put that keen edge on what we had been doing — even the
two days of training in close-order combat with bayonets. (If the
country's survival depended on my skill in hand-to-hand combat, it
was in *big* trouble.)

Our staging area was Moffatt Field, a lighter-than-air station on
the coast a few miles south of San Francisco. Eight-man tents were
already pitched and galleys manned to prepare our food. We were
there three days with nothing to do after our field supplies were
issued. We all got field packs and extra clothing and somehow, I
ended up being issued a Browing automatic rifle which I carried
throughout my tour in the Solomons. Even had a couple of oppor-
tunties to fire it at the enemy. More on that later.

Getting outfitted for overseas took less than half a day; the rest
of the time, two and a half days, was spent waiting. Of course, we
didn't know how long we had to wait, so time hung heavy. No training, no drill, no duties. The third day there, we were given liberty;
we could take liberty buses into Oakland or San Francisco. I had $6
left until payday — not really enough to do much on liberty — so I
shouldered in on one of the many crap games going on in the tents.
My six bucks lasted about an hour, so I stayed in the area that night
and wrote letters.

Reveille came at 0500 the next morning, an hour earlier than
usual. We mustered 15 minutes later and were told to chow down
(eat breakfast) immediately, pack all our gear, and be ready for

"further transfer" by 0730. While we were packing, a passenger train rolled down the tracks that ran adjacent to the area. There must have been a hundred coach cars, some of them already filled with sailors; someone said that many of the cars on the tail end were for freight, about 30 of them. The midsection of the train came to a halt very close to the staging area and we were ordered to "mount up" about 0830; the train pulled out a half-hour later. The damn thing traveled about a hundred yards and stopped! We had to sit in that immobile train for over five hours. Word finally came down that one of the cars or an engine had jumped the tracks! After a winch-car came and got us back on track — and repaired the damaged rail — we were off once again to the war. Our immediate destination, less than an hour away, was the rail yard at one of the piers near downtown San Francisco. What a day!! I'll never forget it. We were finally ordered to dismount, form ranks, and march about a quarter of a mile to the troop transport tied up at the pier, the USS *Wharton.*

Looking back, we must have presented quite a picture: Hundreds of sailors, all dressed in dress blue uniforms, wearing leggins, and carrying a full field pack with a helmet attached. A few of us carried weapons. Police were there to stop traffic while we marched to the ship. Civilians gathered at the curbs and watched us, unsmiling. Some waved to us and more than few cried softly. In retrospect, it must have been a grim sight: Hundreds of sailors outfitted with full field gear, some packing combat weapons — and over three-fourths of those fearless warriors under 21 years of age.

At the gangplank of the *Wharton,* we were given a slip of paper that told us where to go, how to get there, and our billet number. Members of the crew were stationed at points along the way to direct us. I've never seen that many men so quiet. Don't know how many of us were transported that trip, but a reasonable guess would be close to 2,000 plus the ship's crew.

I had never been on a transport before so had never given any thought to what the accommodations might be. When I saw where I was going to be for who knows how long, the stark reality of what was happening scared me half to death. Our outfit was quartered below decks, at least three decks below the main deck, well below the waterline. Tier after tier of bunks filled each compartment, from floor to ceiling (oops, that's deck to overhead), with about 30 vertical inches of sleeping space between bunks; the aisle between the

tiers of bunks was no wider than three feet. The 30 inches of sleeping
space was so close that some of the heavier guys didn't even have
room to turn over! If they were so inclined, they had to get out of
the bunk to do so. We didn't know where our seabags were but
assumed they were in one of the holds. Each man was assigned a
small locker located nearby. We had been ordered to have toilet articles and extra clothing in our field packs which were stowed in an
orderly fashion along one bulkhead of our compartment. Along one
bulkhead was the urinal, a 50-foot long trough running with sea
water; along the opposite bulkhead was another trough fitted with
seats, seats placed so close that you were almost touching buttocks
with the guy next to you. No room on a troop transport for modesty;
nature will prevail! In the center were the wash basins. The showers
were in an adjacent compartment. The basins had fresh water for
the first few days but when it got in short supply, it was replaced with
salt water, as were the showers. This was the era before the advent
of electric shavers, which made shaving a torturous event because
the whiskers had to be literally raked off ; no one could shave with
cold sea water without spilling blood every time. There were only a
dozen or so showerheads, so the line for the shower was always long.
Storebought soap wouldn't lather in salt water; it just gummed up,
so we were issued big brown blocks of "salt water soap." It came in
chunks of stuff that looked like what my grandmother used to make
using ashes and lye. She called it "lye soap" and so did we. Salt water
soap did lather a little bit but was harsh, smelled terrible, and
burned the tender areas, but it did make you feel clean (sticky as
hell, but still clean). Shower space was so limited that the ship had
a dozen or more four-inch water hoses rigged up on deck for two
hours every morning in order for more men to shower. Quite a sight:
a couple of hundred naked sailors pushing and shoving, trying to get
a piece of brown soap or get under a salt water hose to wash off.

*   *   *

The ship shoved off about six in the afternoon — an unforget-
table experience. Everyone who could get on deck watched San
Francisco, Alcatraz, San Leandro, and Mill Valley slide by. The
ship's personnel were trying to make our departure as gala an affair
as they could, so the ship's band played somewhere near the quarter
deck. Just after we slipped under the Golden Gate Bridge out to sea,
they played the number one song on the Lucky Strike Hit Parade
that week, "Harbor Lights." By that time it was dusk and we saw

the lights on the bridge and in the harbor being turned on. I thought about that sight and that song many times over the next few months.

I spent only one night in my bunk in the bowels of the ship because it was hot, crowded, smelly, and loud. Actually, "bowel" describes our quarters very well! Imagine hundreds of men in a tiny space without adequate ventilation (and before air conditioning) where some snored, some talked in their sleep and/or had nightmares, and all passed gas to varying degrees and tunes. You have never had a nightmare until you have experienced a night like that, wide awake. For the rest of the "cruise" I spent every night on deck with a blanket and a pillow — and I had lots of company. I had to get away from the heat, the stink, and the noise, of course, but for the first time in my life, I was genuinely afraid. I didn't want to drown in a place like that. We all knew that this ship, the *Wharton,* had been hit by a Jap torpedo on its last trip out, right on the bow, but it was a dud — didn't explode. Knowing this, if I had to die, I wanted it to be in the wide open spaces, not in anything's bowels. Yecht.

*   *   *

Most of the troops in transit had no assignemnts and nothing to do for the more than three weeks that we were aboard. There were so many men aboard, the chow lines were unbelievable. We were fed from four different locations; long lines had already formed at each place when reveille sounded, and many guys immediately formed up for the lunch line just as soon as they finished breakfast — and the same for dinner that night. It was a late breakfast and early dinner; there was no noon meal. My unit was lucky, not from a chow point of view, but because we didn't have to deal with idleness and inactivity; we were assigned to work with the deck force, scrubbing decks every morning and doing sailor-like things (chip paint, paint, stand gun watches, etc.). Never thought I would look forward to work like that but it was sure preferable to just standing or sitting in a chow line all day long.

*   *   *

When we had a gun watch that fell at chow time, we had to go to the chief master-at-arms shack (office) and get an "early chow" chit. With that, we either ate early or went to the head of the line. It was worth standing a four-hour watch in preference to the hour to hour and a half standing in the chow line. During my first week aboard, I had the noon (12 to 4) watch, so went to the master-at-arms shack for my early chow chit. The office was empty, so I stood there waiting for a few minutes, during which time I couldn't help but see the box on the desk containing the early chow chits. I waited a little longer and when nobody came, I reached over and got a double handful of those chits, put them in my pockets, and headed for the chow line—and for the rest of the trip, I did not spend a single minute in a chow line; I walked up to the head of the line, presented my chit, and filled my tray. I've often wondered what would have happened if I had been caught. The brig, I feel sure.

After a week or so, the ship put into American Samoa, dropped anchor and stayed there a couple of days. Nobody went ashore except a couple of small work parties. That was tough; we were close enough to see activity on the beach but that was all we could do, just watch. The day before we upped-anchor, our outfit was called together and given small-boat assignments; some of us were named coxswain (boat operator), some engineer, and some bow-hook (crew). While we were being briefed, the landing craft aboard the ship were lowered into the water. Each crew went aboard its assigned craft and was instructed by an old salt for about 15 minutes. Once finished, he went back aboard the transport and we were left to "practice"; we made runs to and from the beach (but we didn't go ashore) and we made practice loading runs to and from the ship. They were good practice runs and we did have some fun. See? The war wasn't too tough, was it?

*   *   *

Until our stop in Samoa, our transport had been traveling with one other ship, a tender of some kind, and had three destroyer escorts, but when we left Samoa, three more ships joined the convoy accompanied by three additional destroyers. We still didn't know where we were going, but the scuttlebutt was wild. We all thought it would be combat. A little over a week out of Samoa, probably the first week of August, we were standing a gun watch when we discovered at dawn that the convoy had split; we were no longer a part of a large convoy. We were alone with the supply ship and one destroyer. Sure is a lonesome feeling. Naked, really. A couple of days later, the *Wharton* dropped anchor off the coast of one of the New Hebrides islands, Esperito Santo.

New Hebrides

I rather suspect that we were originally slated to make the initial landing in the Solomons but that the orders had been changed en route in favor of a back-up supply station. Whatever the reason, those of us assigned to the landing craft manned them and started putting the troops ashore, then the supplies.

Since the net depot was separate and apart from the rest of the Navy's mission there, our commanding officer selected a site about a mile down the beach from the rest of the operation. It was a beautiful spot, everything you would expect a copra plantation to look like. We started putting up tents while the plantation manager's natives put up a thatched roof building for us to use as a galley and mess hall. We had wooden decking in our tents and crushed coral sidewalks. It was one of the prettiest spots I have ever seen. Our living area, complete with its transplanted exotic jungle flowers, looked like something out of *Southern Living*.

I didn't get to do any work on our new homesite; the boat crews worked from dawn 'til after dark unloading supplies. We knew what cargo our boats were taking on and where it had to be off-loaded on the beach. For instance, each hold had, primarily, one type of cargo: food, ammo, machinery, construction supplies, arms, etc. Ashore, there were landing sites for each particular item: Food went to one dump, machinery to another, etc.

After the unloading was complete, I got my first lesson in thievery, "How to Steal Anything and Everything on a Grand Scale." In civilian life and in the peacetime Navy it would have been grand theft, a felony, but under these extreme conditions, it was being expeditious, getting the job done under the most adverse conditions. And this knowledge and expertise was to later come in handy.

All the units were expected to be shipshape in 48 hours, even before the distribution system was functional, so we got our supplies the best way we could: we raided the supply dumps. "Midnight Requisition," it was called in some circumstances. As you can well imagine, everything was chaos; anything and everything we wanted for our depot had to be secured with a chit—or requisition—and when we finally found an officer who could issue it, we then had to have another signed chit from some other place. Confusion, confusion. Finally, in desperation, one of our old seadog sailors—regular Navy—came up with what proved to be a real winner. First, he was able to get a stencil-making machine. What he did was easy: he made a stencil with letters about three inches high that read NET AND BOOM. The rest of the procedure was simple: Half-a-dozen sailors would go to a particular dump—all of which were huge, not only in circumference but also in height. Tons of everything it took to build a small city. Raiding a supply dump worked this way: a couple of the guys would saunter up to the Marine guards and start a conversation telling the Marines about who they were (*Net and Boom*) and tell them that we were looking for specified items that were *marked* for our outfit. Meanwhile, the other guys were on the other side of the dump, stenciling NET AND BOOM on anything and everything we thought we might need or use! Most of the stuff in crates was labeled with its contents but a lot of it was not; it was marked only with invoice or job-lot numbers and letters. We usually put everything we purloined to good use, even the stuff in the unlabeled crates. The one exception was a crate of Navy issue pajamas for the sick bay. Ultimately, we utilized most of them as substitutes for dungarees when the ship's store supplies ran low.

I was surprised that this system worked so well, but it always did—and as time went by, we became more and more expert at it. During that first week we got (or stole) a truck, a jeep, a reefer (walk-in cold storage food locker and freezer), a couple of tons of all kinds of food products, especially canned fruits, juices, etc. Never once were we questioned; every time we established that we were NET AND BOOM and that there were things in this dump that were marked for us, the Marine guard said, "Okay, go and get it."

Fortunately, none of them ever sampled the freshness of the stencil paint.

*   *   *

The day we arrived on the island, I was part of the scouting party sent to look for a campsite, and it was I who had seen the plantation from the ship before we went ashore. The chief was interested, so once ashore, I was able to take the chief and the scouting party there. That particular spot was really quite beautiful, something you would expect to see in a movie like *South Pacific*. The

plantation house looked like a small palace to me; serving atten-
dants were everywhere. Tonkinese they called them because they
came from somewhere in the Gulf of Tonkin in Southeast Asia
where labor was plentiful and cheap.

I don't know how many acres of coconut trees were on the plantation, but there had to be several hundred. Only natives from the
Tonkin Gulf were in evidence to work the copra. Many blacks were
native to the New Hebrides, but they did not work; they were tribal.
Theirs was a community or society that could hardly be classified as
civilized. They must have been subsidized by the British because
they were always idle but appeared to be well fed. They were mostly
naked, only wore a loincloth and sometimes a shirt of some kind.
Funny looking guys (we never saw a black female), they always carried a spear or lance of some kind, like they were ready to do battle
but they were really quite docile. Their funny looks came from the
betel nut and lime that they seemed to be addicted to. The betel nut
was a mild narcotic that kept them on a floating kind of high as long
as they took it. They dipped it in lime constantly like my Aunt Tinnie
used to dip snuff. It turned their teeth jet black and the inside of their
mouths a bright cherry red.

*   *   *

The Tonkinese slave-like quarters were on the beach not too far
from the main house. The plantation owner or manager was a
Frenchman who was delighted to have us as neighbors. He volunteered his workers for whatever we needed them to do. Their first
and only task was to build us a thatched-roof chow hall/galley, a
building big enough to prepare food for and feed 120 men. Six men
put it up in one day, complete with a crushed coral floor and bloom-
ing hibiscus bushes on all sides. The following night we spent in our
tents at the new campsite, very close to the plantation house.

When reveille sounded that first morning, we went outside and
were greeted by a rather unusual sight on the beach: It was low tide
and there, well below the high water mark, were a dozen or so
Tonkinese workers, pants dropped and or skirts hiked, all squatting
on the beach for their "morning's morning" totally unconcerned
with privacy and lacking in modesty. This morning ritual, with the
workers coming and going, went on for about an hour. I don't suppose they had a sanitary facility other than the ocean; if they did,
I never saw it. That same scene greeted us each morning.

*   *   *

About the middle of August, a cargo ship put into the anchorage there at the Naval Operating Base and called for lighters (which is what some of our landing craft were called). The beachmaster sent us, with no special instruction, to offload the cargo she carried. It was quite a shock to learn that our cargo was human: Marines, the walking wounded from the Solomon invasion. The ship also carried the seriously wounded, but they were being taken back to the hospital at Pearl Harbor. The ones we took on were suffering from minor wounds; they were sent to the field hospital in New Hebrides to convalesce, then they could rejoin their units when they were healed enough. They were a bunch of tough guys. The medics referred to them as the "walking wounded" as far as transport was concerned, but most of them, it seemed to me, were walking in spite of being wounded. The chief corpsman who was the Non-Commissioned Officer (NCO) in charge briefed us on the condition of the men before they were offloaded to our boats; he said that those being left in the New Hebrides to recover were considered "minor wounds," those who would be fit to return to duty in 30 days or less. If these guys had minor wounds, I'm sure glad I didn't get to go aboard the ship to see the seriously wounded! There must be a pretty close connection between how bad a Marine is hurt and how bad he *thinks* he's hurt. One lance corporal I talked to on the way to the beach later went AWOL before the stitches were removed from his arm and side where a Jap grenade had scratched him up pretty good. He was caught stowed away on a cargo whip on its way to Guadalcanal with ammo and aviation gasoline; the poor guy was afraid his platoon would think he was goldbricking. Most of the Marines were giving the medics a bad time about keeping them there; they all wanted to go back to their outfits.

It was quite a hospital these guys came to: Eight-man tents — about 50 of them — had been pitched in a coconut grove not far from our base camp. There had not been time (or it had not been thought of) to put wooden decking down for the floors; the tents were pitched on the grass. There were three latrines — screen-in four-holers — and a larger tent that served as a field kitchen. No mess hall; the men sat on the ground or went back to their tents. Pretty primitive. Maybe it was better in combat! Since the field hospital was nearby and we were hungry for the straight dope about combat, some of us made several visits there. Sure didn't realize it at the time, but our visits were excellent therapy for the wounded; they needed someone outside to talk to about the hell they had been through and we needed to hear the combat stories because we never expected to be in combat. Even though it didn't work out that way for us, we were a little bit more prepared for the Solomons than we would have been otherwise.

The Marines told us that the invasion of Guadalcanal was a piece of cake. When they hit the beach after the cruisers, destroyers, and planes had shelled and bombed it, not a single shot was fired during the invasion — not by the Japs and not by the Marines. The Marines found "nobody home" but a hot breakfast was already prepared and on the table ready to serve. (Some Marines even stopped long enough to have a quick bite but were not impressed with boiled rice being the breakfast staple.) What the Marines learned was that the Japanese fighting force was concentrated on the island of Tulagi, twenty miles across the channel from Guadalcanal and that the Jap high command was building an airfield on Guadalcanal for their bombers. The "fighting force" the Marines faced were civilian construction workers and a few armed sailors.

Tulagi was just the opposite: It was a naval operating base on a good harbor. Two islets, Gavutu and Tanambogo, were attached to the main base by causeways — and the whole place was heavily fortified. The fighting there was fierce; it took about 30 hours to secure — and it was costly: 144 Marines were killed and another 200 wounded.

The only casualty from Guadalcanal was a Marine who had a deep gash on his hand; he was "wounded" trying to open a coconut by hacking on the end of it with a machete or with his bayonet — depending on who was telling the story at the time (we heard several versions). The tough husk deflected the blade, sinking it deep into his other hand!

We got the full poop on what combat was like from the guys who were wounded at Tulagi. It was a tough operation and set the stage for what to expect as the Navy and Marines island-hopped their way toward the Sea of Japan. The landing took place just after sundown so that the Marines could utilize the darkness to cover their going over the open ground at the seaplane base on Gavutu — but it didn't happen.

The last salvo from the ship shelling the base hit a fuel dump which exploded and burned for hours, silhouetting the Marines. That one fire was responsible for most of the casualties in the Tulagi raid. Japanese losses were really heavy; they suffered 700 dead out of an 800-man force. Less than a half dozen prisoners were taken, and those only for intelligence purposes. Another 50 or so Jap survivors swam to safety on Florida Island, about a mile away (at one point) from Gavutu.

Solomon Islands: First Stop

About a week after we brought the first Marine casualties ashore, our CO came roaring into base in his stolen jeep and yelled at the chief to "Muster the men!" Our new orders were short and sweet: "proceed immediately to Naval Base Cactus." We guessed that we were on our way to the Solomons! We had to be ready to board at 0600 the next morning — and I almost didn't get to go!

A week earlier, another sailor and I were told to take the motor whaleboat, go up the river to a spring and fill all our water casks with fresh water. The water supply used by the plantation didn't pass the sanitation inspection, so the only way we could drink it was after a heavy treatment with iodine. Two things happen to iodine-treated water: It tasted so bad it was difficult to swallow — and after a couple of drinks, guess what? Diarrhea. That's why I was trying to open up that green coconut in the first place. We were told that the milk in a green coconut was cool and sweet and that the forming substance on the inside of the shell was also sweet and soft and even tasted a little bit like warm ice cream. Anyway, while my shipmate was filling a cask, I was working on a green coconut with my hunting knife. (All shore sailors then carried knives, legally.) Mine was sharp enough to shave the hairs off my forearm, so a coconut husk shouldn't have been any problem — but it turned out to be a major one. That sharp knife slipped off the slick green coconut and cut across the top of my left index finger all the way to the bone, pretty much like what happened to the Marine at Guadalcanal. By the time we got back to base six hours later, it was infected. Next morning, the finger was swollen and festered. We had a hospital corpsman with our outfit, a second-class petty officer whose name was "Doc," which was also the name of 99 percent of all the medics in the military. Doc cut the nail back so the wound would drain and he used a lot of sulfa powder on it — but it only got worse. By the time we got orders to go to the Solomons, a red stripe beginning at my finger was running up the inside of my arm toward my armpit. Doc was going to take me over to the field hospital and dump me that afternoon, but I talked him out of it. We made a deal; if I did exactly as he told me on the way to the Solomons, and if he thought the wound was better when we got there, I could stay. If not, I would be left on the ship and evacuated back to the New Hebrides, immediately. I didn't have any choice but to agree — so those were the conditions when we boarded the transport the next morning.

We had precious little time to pack up and be ready to move; we took our sea bags, ditty bags, full field packs, helmets, and what few weapons had been issued — that was all. For parties unknown (but more than likely the Frenchman), we left behind as beautiful and well-equipped a military camp as you will ever see, complete with cots and mattresses in the tents, a galley complete with all cooking utensils, several hundred pounds of perishables in the reefer, and vast quantities of canned and dried foods. That Frenchman was awfully anxious to cooperate with us.

I don't remember the name of the ship we boarded, but she was carrying cargo and had the capability of transporting a sizable troop load; we were the only passengers aboard, however. Once aboard we were told that we were going to the Solomon Islands — which was certainly no surprise. This trip, however, was a far cry from being one of several thousand troops on the USS *Wharton*. Transit quarters on this one were large staterooms normally used to quarter senior officers. For our small contingent, six men per stateroom — except for me; I was taken straight to the sick bay and put under the charge of another medic, a first class petty officer named (you guessed it) "Doc."

The first thing the two medics did was to put me on a medication every four hours — probably sulfa — and had me soak my hand in hot epsom-salt water for thirty minutes every two hours. I did this religiously, from reveille at 0530 till bedtime, usually close to midnight. Sitting there in that sick bay all day every day, I read two very good novels, *King's Row* and *The Rains Came*. By sundown the third day, I had it made; the red stripe that had started up my arm was gone and there was no more drainage — the infection was gone!

Throughout that voyage, though, I was bugged constantly by one nagging question: What am I going to do for shoes?

The black ones I bought in Chicago were in pretty bad shape; they had gotten a lot of hard wear on the transport and in the New Hebrides. Even with moderate wear, they wouldn't last more than another month. Was I going to have to spend the rest of the war barefooted?

Since I would be going ashore the next morning, I thought I should go in clean. We had no idea of what kind of sanitary facilities awaited us. I was in the shower, all soaped up, when the explosion came. BOOM! The concussion knocked me to the tiled floor of the shower. Almost immediately, the voice on the loudspeaker shouted, "General Quarters; man your battle stations!"

I shot out of the shower, still wet and soapy, pulling my clothes on as I headed for the deck. The explosion had come from a depth charge dropped by a destroyer-escort that was close in to our port side; the depth gauge had been set too shallow, so the ships got more of the impact than the Jap sub did. What happened was that a Japanese sub was following, directly astern and very close to our ship. Her intent was not to sink us but to follow us, hoping that we would lead her to a rendezvous where bigger and better targets would be available. We never did see the sub; it had been picked up on sonar. Within a matter of minutes, our destroyer escorts were crisscrossing the area, dropping more depth charges. No kill; the Jap got away.

*   *   *

It was after dark when the ship pulled into the bay at Tulagi. Motor whaleboats came out to pick us up, then returned to pick up our gear. It was late at night when we got ashore, close to midnight. Someone from the Naval Operating Base—of which we were to become a part—had us fall in, gave us a short welcoming talk, and told us to "Follow me" to a billet for the night. He then told us that we would be given duty assignments and permanent billets the next day. It was a pitch-black night, no moon and no stars; we could not see anything, not even the man in front of us, so we were told to grab the shirttail of the "man on your left and follow the leader."

We ended up in a fairly large building on the bay in what was once a trading post or store of some kind. It was now empty except for the bunks that had been built in. There was space enough to accommodate the 120 men in our outfit. The bunks were built in on the inner walls and cots had been set up in the middle of the room. When we went inside, the blackout curtains were drawn so that we would have enough light from a couple of small candles to pick a bunk and get in it. With the light, we saw that there were two extra men with us in that building. They were Marines, that's all we knew; we didn't know where they came from nor where they went after the Japanese destroyer finished shelling the area less than an hour later.

Not long after we had bedded down for the night, all hell broke loose: A Jap ship had put its nose right in the entrance to the bay, then opened up with everything she had. With the first salvo, everybody hit the deck and then headed outside to look for a safe place to take cover. But only seconds after the salvo, as we were getting the hell outa there, there was also another explosion, a gunshot inside the building, but it was small potatoes compared to what was being thrown at us from the outside. We blindly vacated the building and somehow found cover. The shelling lasted less than a half hour — maybe fifteen minutes — but it seemed like hours! Our sleeping quarters weren't hit but a number of the other buildings were.

When the "All Clear" sounded, we went back to our transient billet to go back to bed. The blackout curtains were drawn again because some of the cots in the middle of the room had been turned over as we rushed out. The first thing we saw amongst the jumble of bedding was Dave Enders, one of our guys; he was lying on the floor with a gunshot wound to the head. Actually, the 45-caliber slug had blown half his head off. His death was instantaneous, so there was little blood. But bits of bone, brains, and hair were scattered all over one side of the room. We never found out what happened; we could only surmise that one of the two Marines who came in to bunk with us pulled his sidearm in panic when that first salvo went off, and in so doing his weapon fired accidentally, the wild shot hitting Dave as he was getting up from the cot. It had to be something like that because those two Marines were the only persons in that room who wore sidearms — and neither of them came back after the shelling was over. We put Dave's body on a stretcher, covered him with his white Navy blanket and left him at the guard shack until dawn the next morning. Four of us carried his body to the cemetery where a pre-dug grave was waiting as the temporary burial place. Our CO told us that his parents would be notified that Dave had been killed in action — and actually, he was.

*   *   *

Dave Enders' body was the first I had ever seen not embalmed and in a casket. He was not dressed in a suit and tie, hands folded, and hair combed. Dave had on dirty dungarees, socks but no shoes. When we got to the temporary cemetery to bury him the next morning, rigor mortis had set in, but he still had that faint smile on his face, not a smile exactly, but more of a very pleasant look. There was a hole about an inch above his left eyebrow where the slug entered; it took the back of his head off when it exited. It was not a pleasant sight. I had a lot to learn about death, especially about death the hard way, like getting blown to pieces in combat.

Just about the only death I had ever seen up to this point was in the movies except for my Grandpa; he died of old age at our house when I was a kid, but I didn't see it; I was told to "go outside and play" while the old man fought for those final few gulps of air. Earlier, I heard Dr. Stewart tell my father that Grandpa had pneumonia and that his lungs were filling up, that he was actually drowning in his own body fluids. Don't know why they wouldn't let me stay with Grandpa while he was dying because I spent a lot of time with him while he lived with us that last year. He was in his eighties and pretty grumpy, but we got along fine most of the time.

Grandpa could do a lot of swell things for an old man who only had one arm. He was a young boy during the Civil War. Once when he was cleaning a loaded musket, it fired and blew his let arm off at the shoulder. Sure didn't seem to slow him down very much. He never told me much about his childhood, but he did talk about the time he married my grandma (whom I never knew) and how he courted her. At the time they were courting, Grandpa couldn't read or write. Miss Bobbie (he always called her that) had a college degree. By the time they married, she was teaching him his "letters." When their children were old enough to go to school, Grandpa was the school teacher! He didn't stop there; he "read" for the law, passing his bar exam administered by a transient federal judge. Grandpa said they talked and the judge asked lots of questions mostly. When he came to live with us, he brought his Royal typewriter along, probably a 1900 vintage. Amazing old man (mean as hell, but amazing); he could type 40 words-per-minute using that one hand!

He was a pretty good lawyer, too, both in private practice (he liked criminal cases) and in public service as a county judge, but one of his contributions to society had nothing to do with the law; it was a knife/fork utensil that a one-armed person could use to cut up and eat a steak without any help. Here's what he did: he took a file to the blacksmith and had him heat it till it could be beaten pretty flat and then bent (on the flat side) into a curve on one end — which was then fashioned with tines; the outer edge at the curve was honed razor-sharp for cutting by using a rocking motion. Within twenty years, his utensil was being used by amputees all over the country. The man who marketed it got rich — but not Grandpa; he never bothered to file the patent papers.

What I'm saying is that up to this point in my life, my only real encounter with death had been with Grandpa. While he died in our front bedroom, I "played" under the window outside.

Where I really learned about death (before I came and lived in the midst of it) was in the movies. Everybody knew that when Gary Cooper or Clark Gable or Victor Mature died, they would do so heroically, like gentlemen. How many times have we seen our hero shot by an Indian or an enemy soldier that he didn't die just beautifully? He grunted a little when the slug or arrow hit him, dropped to his knees, then fell to the ground and rolled over on his back. There was always this heroic expression on his face, then a trickle of blood would ooze from the corner of his mouth. Always, there was a final shudder or the "death throes" before he expired, looking so peaceful but still in command of the situation, even in death. And in the movies, it was almost always men that died, seldom women.

Same thing with airplane crashes in the movies; no matter how bad the crash, the pilot, or hero (usually one and the same), was always in one piece and lived long enough to say or do something brave before the trickle of blood from the corner of the mouth and the final shudder. Kinda made you feel good all over. Sad, sure, but good!

                    *   *   *

War correspondents and photographers contribute to the deception as to how men and women actually die in combat and plane crashes. Dead soldiers in combat — almost always enemy soldiers — are scanned by the camera and always to places where the bodies are all in one piece. How many times do we see a mutilated or dismembered body? Almost never. We never see bodies at the scene of a plane crash; only the mangled airplane itself is shown. I'm sure that correspondents and photographers — and their newspapers — would say that it would be insensitive and in poor taste to show mangled and dismembered bodies however they were killed, even the enemy. And they are right. Even though death is realistic, some things are just too gruesome to show graphically or describe literally. Suffice it to say, this is why kids grow up thinking that soldiers and airmen die heroically and in one piece, usually with one neat bullet hole that leads to a vital organ; the "victims" know that they are dying, so they make a class act of it. Sailors always die in one piece, you know; they are just blown overboard to drown, but not always; in rare instances, some do have that ooze of blood from the mouth and die with smiles on their wet faces.

In training, they taught us about the velocity of certain projectiles, all the way from 22-caliber to 20-millimeter, but they were never specific about what the size and speed of a bullet will do to the human body. Did you know that a short burst (10 rounds) from a 30-caliber machine gun can cut a human body in half? And that the same burst from a 50-caliber can dismember and decapitate a body, sending arms and legs, bits and pieces, in all directions? None of us sailors had been prepared for this kind of war; maybe the Marines were but not us. Where do you find dead soldiers all in one piece with maybe a little blood on a piece of clothing? We didn't get to see many of them where we were; we saw many more torn bodies and body parts than we did whole bodies.

* * *

When I returned home after my tour in the Solomon Islands, the most frequently asked question was, "What was it like in combat?" Hardly a day of my leave went by that I wasn't asked that question in one form or another. It was a tough question because I was not supposed to know what it was like in combat because we were officially classified as noncombatants! We had been in the combat zone where the Marines and the Japs were fighting on all sides — and in the air. We were on the three-mile-by-five-mile stretch of land that was surrounded by the Japanese army and where her navy sailed up and down the Slot like the U.S. Navy didn't even exist, where most nights they steamed up from Rabual and Port Moresby, almost at will, to land troops and supplies. They commanded not only the land and the sea, but their bombers flew over our little portion of the island and bombed us twice a day, every day, for weeks and months on end. Their warships even came in at night, up close, and shelled Henderson Field, mostly. As their intelligence-gathering network improved, they began shelling Marine gun emplacements and other strategic targets as well.

Getting shelled by enemy warships wasn't at all unusual and became almost routine. Most of the time, we hit the foxholes when the shelling started but as time went by, more and more of us took less and less precaution when the shooting started.

"After all," we reasoned, "those ships are trying to destroy the airstrip and planes. They don't give a hoot about a few Higgins boats and a few sailors that call themselves an Operating Base."

So we stayed in our bunks and many times slept right through an attack from the sea.

A couple or three such attacks did get our attention, the shelling attacks from Japanese battlewagons firing 18-inch guns. When they came in to shell, the exploding gunfire from the ship was so loud and the concussion so great that we were literally blown out of our bunks. Shaving mirrors and what little glass we had around was broken. Running from tent to foxhole was like running a new kind of obstacle course; when a salvo was fired, the concussion threw you to the ground. Then when you got up, the concussion from the exploding salvo on the airstrip threw you down again.

Even though we knew the sailors were not a target, the noise and concussion alone was one of the war's more frightening experiences. The sky lighted up like midday a fraction of a second before we heard the gunfire, then we felt the intense heat of the rounds on our bare flesh as they passed overhead on the way to the target — then another bright flash when it hit the target a quarter of a mile away. We felt the heat of the shells because the ship was in so close to shore that the shells on their way to the airstrip were traveling low, on a flat trajectory. One would occasionally clip a frond from a palm tree — and that is a *very* low trajectory!

Another phenomenon of the war was that the folks back home knew more, much more, about what was going on in the Solomon Islands than we who were there in the midst of it. We assumed that a sea battle was in progress when we saw lightning-like flashes in the distance, then heard sounds like faint claps of thunder. Sometimes at night we heard battle-like noises coming from somewhere deep in the jungle and assumed that the Japs were trying to overrun a Marine position. We didn't have newspapers or radio; what little we knew about our part of the war was what we could actually see and what little we were told. We didn't believe most of what we heard unless it came firsthand from a reliable source, like our CO; anything else was scuttlebutt, pure fiction after it had been repeated a couple of times. There were times when we got to read newspaper clippings that someone had gotten from home. It was a strange feeling because what we read sounded like another war in another place; rarely could we relate anything the stories said to where we were or what we were doing. We knew we were in a pretty tough situation but had no idea it was as tough as the newspapers reported.

"Does this mean that this kind of stuff has been going on *here* to *us?* They must be writing about somebody else's war."

I guess you could say, loosely speaking, that we had been "in combat" but it sure was different from the sort of combat those Marines went through out there in the jungle.

*   *   *

For the first four months of our duty in the Solomons, we could not write home and tell the folks where we were; all we could say was that we were "somewhere in the Pacific" or some similar term. Letters were censored very carefully with a razor blade. Any word, phrase, or sentence that gave even a hint about where we were or what we were doing was cut out. Some of the guys got cute and tried to write home in code words or some other covert way, but the attempt was usually so amateurish that the censor simply returned the shredded letter to the writer. It wasn't long, however, before most of our families knew where we were without our having to use but one of two words: yes or no.

We hadn't been in the Solomons a week before our Greek cook, Tony, got a letter from his wife. Knowing that her letter would not be censored, she told Tony to write her and begin the first sentence of the second paragraph with the word yes or no. If he was not in the Solomons, he was to begin that paragraph with something like, "No, I did not receive your letter about mom being in the hospital" or some such similar sentence. "Yes, I did get the letter about the insurance premium" if he was.

It wasn't a month before 90 percent of the families had a code very similar to that. Our families could talk about our part of the war, but we couldn't. It was November of 1942, about the time it looked like the Japs might retake the island, that we could write home and say, "Guess what, I'm on Guadalcanal and am having a very nice time in this tropical paradise," or some such drivel.

The reason we could at long last reveal where we were was not for our benefit, but for our families. If the Solomons should fall, the Brass thought the folks back home should have a little bit of a cushion to take the shock. Little did they know that they were not quite up to what was going on in that respect. Many newspapers said something like, "our own Joe Blow is believed to be in the Solomon Islands, taking part in the fierce fighting on Guadalcanal."

*   *   *

Back to the shore-sailors' war: Right after we buried Dave, I hightailed it over to the Marine quartermaster outfit on the island

and asked to see the NCO in charge. A grizzled old gunnery sergeant came out of the office.

"Yeah?"

I talked and he listened. I told him about my Navy-issue shoes, what happened at Navy Pier, and about the shopping spree for shoes in Chicago.

"And now I'm here with this pair of shoes that are about wore out. Do the Marines have anything at all that I can wear that will get me through duty here without making me a cripple?"

They did. Gunny went over to a shelf loaded with combat boots, got a pair and threw them to me. I looked at the size: 12 N.

"Shit."

"Now don't go gettin' your bowels in an uproar, sailor boy, just listen to what I'm gonna tell ya. Put on two pairs of socks, then put them boots on. Find a big tub, big enough to get both feet in up to the tops of the boots. Then build a fire and heat the water 'til it's almost too hot to stick your hand in. Take it off the fire and find yourself a nice comfortable place to sit 'cause you're gonna be there until the water is cool, maybe one, two hours, then get up and go back to duty, but *do not take the boots off until they are completely dry,* even if you hafta sleep in 'em tonight."

The gunny sergeant was right. When the boots were dry, they had shrunk or something. In any event, the boots were actually molded to my feet. Never have had anything that fit better or was more comfortable. We wore out a pair of combat boots in about two months, so I had to go through this procedure two more times.

*   *   *

Our outfit was always known as *"Net and Boom";* we were trained in all phases of manufacture, laying, tending, etc. When we arrived in the New Hebrides, however, we did not find our nets in any of the cargo unloaded there — which made us think that they had gone on to the combat zone and there we would probably be following soon. Not so — our nets were not put ashore in New Hebrides and if they were in the Solomons, we didn't find them or ever hear of them again. Although our unit name, *"Net and Boom,"* remained the same, from this point on we were a part of the Naval Operating Base.

We didn't stay on Tulagi very long, but it was a pretty good duty while it lasted. We were quartered in a big old house on a point of land on the far side of the bay. The house had already been gutted by the Japanese, so we fixed it up with built-in bunks around the inside frame that had once had walls. To keep the water out when it rained, we had a sort of roll-up awning which we let down in bad weather. For evening recreation, there was one big inside room which was boarded in, then covered, so that we could have a lantern or two for light. There was always a poker game going on inside, some of the guys read, etc. I don't see how anyone could stand that room. After 15 minutes inside, clothing was soaked with perspiration and the stench of unwashed bodies, cigarette smoke, and stale sweat was more than I could take. The nights were beautiful in the tropics when the Japs weren't flying around up there, dropping an occasional bomb. Many of us enjoyed the peace and serenity when such a moment was available.

*   *   *

The beat-up old house that was our billet had been, at some time in the past, a very nice tropical residence. Don't know what the inside and outside walls looked like because the Japs had torn them out so that the ocean breeze, when there was one, would flow throughout the house. The floors were of red mahogany, beautiful even in their neglect. Like the other rooms, the kitchen had been stripped, and was an open area; the entire roof and upper structure was supported by the framing. There was one outbuilding — the bathroom. It was aptly named because that was all the building was used for; it contained an oversized bathtub and nothing else. The day we occupied the house, the CO had a sign put on the bathhouse door saying, "Officers' Country." There was some ill feeling among the men about this.

The enlisted men built a shower out in the open space behind the house. There were only two showerheads so we had to stand in line and wait our turn. The shower was supplied with fresh water from the roof runoff into a huge storage tank — perhaps as big as 500 gallons. We used that runoff water not only to drink, but to bathe in as well.

Funny thing happened about that water: We were rarely in the house during the daylight hours so all our activity there was in the dark. I was sent back to the house one morning to do an errand and before I returned to duty drew a big cup of water to drink — but I didn't drink from that tank again. The tank water was the breeding ground for the island's mosquitoes; the cup was *teeming* with larvae.

When I crawled up on the tank, I saw that the protective screen over the hole in the middle of the tank had been moved aside. I replaced it, crawled back down, and returned to my work party. Never did tell anyone about the larvae and felt guilty about it for a while, but nobody got sick. How can you get sick on all that protein?

*   *   *

About the "Officers' Country" bathroom: One day while we were all away on a work party, someone slipped away and dropped a hand grenade in that tub. The resulting blast reconfigured the tub; it then looked like a huge sieve. There was a big investigation and all sorts of hell raised by the CO but the culprit was never found.

*   *   *

Toilet facilities consisted of a platform built over the water complete with an open air Chic Sales four-holer. The incoming and outgoing tides were the flushing device. Our two officers had a similar facility, only theirs was a one-holer. That's what you call luxury; sharing our potty-time with only four out of 160 sailors was what we thought of as semi-private.

*   *   *

Sailors are very resourceful people, at least those I knew were. Take alcohol, for example. When there are 60 men in a group, there are a certain number who are going to have something to drink, come hell or high water. The first thing this group tried was a five-gallon can of 180 proof grain alcohol that had been traded from a submarine that put in overnight for supplies. Torpedoes were powered by alcohol, so there was a lot of it aboard. Problem was, it had been poisoned. Not to worry; these dudes knew how to "cut" the poison out. First, they got unsliced loaves of bread from the galley, cut each end off, and poured the alcohol through the bread; the bread was supposed to strain the poison out — but it didn't. All they got was poisoned alcohol with bread crumbs in it. Next, they got a can of lye and dumped it in the alcohol and stirred it up; the lye was supposed to cut the poison. One positive result: The green dye in the alcohol disappeared. (It was put there to denote its being poison and unfit for human consumption.) It looked pure, so it was sampled: One man took a mouthful, swished it around, then spit it out — and was taken to the main sick bay with a badly burned mouth. That did it; they finally gave up on the denatured alcohol.

(Doc later told me that the lye might have done the job, but he wasn't sure. What he was sure of was that anyone who took a mouthful of 180-proof grain alcohol was going to have a burned mouth, regardless of whether it was poisoned or not.)

The next experiment in making something potent came about a week later. The same guys who got the torpedo juice also came up with several gallons of fruit juice, probably pineapple as I remember, and put it in a five-gallon oak water cask — the kind that held the drinking water in lifeboats. Into this juice, they dumped a couple of pounds of raisins and some dry yeast, then sealed it and put it away to "cook." Sure enough, it worked. They had two of those five-gallon casks hidden in an old warehouse the Japs had built. It had been cooking for a week or so when we had a General Quarters situation on the island. A cargo vessel loaded with foodstuffs put into the bay around a protective bend so that it was safe from the open sea. Originally, the ship was destined for Guadalcanal but a Jap submarine fired three fish at it — and missed. With the help of their escort vessels, they managed to make it to the safety of the harbor. They were afraid to leave because the sub was still out there waiting.

Hence cometh the *Net and Boom*. The decision was made to unload the cargo at Tulagi — and the only people to do the unloading, transporting, and storing the cargo was us! It took 60 men working continuously for 33 hours to empty the ship. We took off 30 minutes to eat and as long as necessary on the john. I've never been so tired in my whole life. The last few hours weren't too bad though. Our boozehounds decided to sample what they dubbed "Jungle Juice" — and fortunately(?), it was ready. The drinking procedure was this: after a truck was loaded, it was headed for the warehouse where we all worked very fast to unload so that we would have a little time to stop by and enjoy a canteen-cup of Jungle Juice before we headed back to the ship. After two stops, several of us were getting pretty high. I don't remember the third stop nor do I remember finishing the unloading. I do remember the hangover. Once I was sober the next morning, I threw up all day and have never in my life had such a hangover — and the headache was excruciating. I'm told that I — and a few others — threw up all over the ship, the cargo, the truck, and the warehouse. We were all put on report and had to go to the Captain's Mast the following day — but the Captain had to postpone the Mast because most of us were too sick to appear. (I threw up every time I stood up or took a drink of water.)

When we did appear, our sentences were the same: We got a horrendous butt-chewing and 30 hours extra duty. How can you do extra duty when you're already working an 18-hour day?

*   *   *

All things considered, we had it pretty good at Tulagi. It was quiet and peaceful except for a shelling from sea every now and then. Compared to Guadalcanal, 20 miles across Ironbottom Sound (so named because of the number of Allied and Japanese ships that had been sunk there), it was duty we later called "pretty soft." True, Jap ships did shell us periodically at night, but there were no Japs on the island and the Jap bombers that flew over every day were on their way to bomb Henderson Field on Guadalcanal. We did work long hours unloading ships (with Marine work parties doing the heavy stuff) and maintaining the Section Base, but we were relatively safe and we ate well.

*   *   *

The Marines assigned to our lighters had been on the initial assault on Tulagi, so we got a first-hand account of what went on. The force that hit Guadalcanal at 7 A.M. the morning of August 7th met no resistance; what they finally encountered there was a small detachment of sailors who carried rusty old rifles and a large force of civilian workers about to finish construction of the airfield, all of whom headed for cover when the first shells and bombs began to fall. The main force of Japanese was on Tulagi — which numbered anywhere from 1,000 to 1,600 men, depending on whom you talked to who was there at the time. Tulagi had been well populated by the British when the Japanese occupied it in May of 1942; it was then the British administrative capital for all of the Solomon Islands — but there were no British there at the time of the invasion. On the day of the invasion, the Marines slated to storm the beach sat on the ship all day and watched while the Jap emplacements were shelled and bombed. They went ashore just after sunset, expecting it to be relatively easy after all the softening up coming from the planes and warships, expecting it to be little more than a mopping-up operation. Wrong. The Japs fell back to the hills and were emplaced in hard-to-get-at caves. When the Marines went ashore, the Japs were well dug in and were ready to fight. It was on this initial assault that we learned the Japanese were not only fanatical, but suicidal as well. The Americans should have known more about the Japanese mind, but we did not. We had to learn it the hard way: On the battlefield, at sea, and in the air.

* * *

One of the prime mistakes the Brass made in planning the invasion of the Solomons was to underestimate the courage and culture of the enemy—especially the culture. Twenty years after the war ended, I was given a firsthand account of what honor and obedience meant to a 17-year-old Japanese boy who had been given the privilege of volunteering his life for the Emperor. Hiroshi was still a student at the military school on Okinawa when he asked to be released from his studies to become a kamikaze pilot, an honor that was not accorded to just anyone. Gaining acceptance as a kamikaze was just as demanding as was acceptance to one of the military academies.

This form of soldiering was born out of desperation when the tide of battle ebbed from the Japanese and flowed toward the Allies. It was a last-ditch effort to stop the American advances up the island chain toward the Japanese homeland. Japanese youths were used to pilot small bomb-loaded planes into American warships and troops transports. Unfortunately, kamikaze flying was not seen by the Imperial Command as an act of desperation or the senseless waste of Japanese youth in its prime, but they were convinced that it was an opportunity for the elite young men of the Empire to serve their Emperor in the finest tradition of a Samurai warrior.

Hiroshi went through a month of flight training, finally soloing and earning his special wings with only six hours of actual flight instruction. He was commissioned and given the badge of his future heroism—a white sash with the Rising Sun embroidered on the center surrounded by a sea of small red stitches; it was to be donned over the leather flight helmet just prior to the ceremonial drinking of sake, the warm wine made from rice, just prior to takeoff on the warrior's one and only flight. The sash, also called "the belt of a thousand stitches," was made by wives and mothers as a humongous prayer for the warrior. Each of the thousand stitches on the belt was made by a different person who said a short prayer for the wearer. These trophies sometimes took months to complete. It was a usual sight in Japan, women on street corners stopping strangers and asking for a stitch and a prayer.

I listened as Hiroshi told me of his training, his hopes, and his wildest dreams for his brief military career—dreams and a career that were never to be realized. The Americans had invaded Okinawa and were slowly taking the island when Hiroshi's call came to serve his Emperor, but before his transportation could reach the airfield, it fell to the Marines. Hiroshi managed to elude capture and was trying to reach the field on foot when he was taken prisoner. All this just a few months before the war was over. In the eyes of the Samurai, of course, he was a disgrace because he did not commit harakiri. He was able, somehow, to rise above it. He didn't tell me how he made the change from one culture to another, but I imagine it made a very interesting story.

Hiroshi told me all this over lunch one day at a small cafe in Koza. I was on a business assignment in Okinawa and had stopped in for Morning Prayer at the small Episcopal church where he was a priest and teacher at the school.

*   *   *

The Japanese soldiers were not only willing to fight for their country, but many like Hiroshi were anxious to die for their Emperor. Surrender was unheard of. The Emperor of Japan was a god, and to die for this god meant an immediate entrance into immortality. Oriental sainthood, I suppose you could call it. And that is exactly what happened to most of the defenders of Tulagi, Gavutu, and Tanambogo during the 30-odd hours of the battle there. Immortality the hard way. The Marines there on the island told us about their killing hundreds of Jap soldiers as they made fanatic, suicidal charges across what had once been a British cricket field. Others fell back to caves in the hills behind the town where all were killed, a cave at a time, with grenades, mortars, and high-explosive TNT charges. Those in the caves who were not killed by the blasts were buried alive. Not a single Jap soldier surrendered. The Marines suffered heavy losses in the fighting for the seaplane base on Gavutu. The Japanese almost turned the tide there with the help of exploding and burning aviation gasoline. The last "softening up" salvo from a cruiser hit a Jap fuel dump just as the main body of Marines hit the beach. The Marines finally made it, but they suffered heavy losses. Only a handful of prisoners were taken; an estimated 50 or more enemy soldiers made it to safety on Florida Island a short distance away.

*   *   *

Before we left Tulagi, a squadron of motor torpedo boats arrived and were tied up at the pier. They were not like any Navy outfit we had ever seen before. Everybody except the duty watch slept until 10 or 11:00 in the morning, then turned-to at 1 P.M., after lunch — which was their breakfast. After working on and readying their boats, they went out on Ironbottom Sound late at night in pursuit of the Japanese ships called "the Tokyo Express" — enemy ships loaded with troops and supplies that were being put ashore on Guadalcanal almost every night. The PT boats (Patrol Torpedo) were pretty effective, but the duty on one was hazardous. They were constructed of plywood and had high-powered diesel marine engines that would hit better than 60 miles per hour on a torpedo run. Besides the torpedoes, their armament consisted of 20-millimeter machine guns (small cannons, really) mounted fore and aft. When they sighted a Jap ship, they would usually sneak in slowly until they were detected, then gun it up to top speed, guns blazing, straight at the enemy craft until the torpedoes were released at short range. Real hazardous duty.

A couple of the guys who were checked out on 20-millimeters went on patrol with them a few times, but I never did. Our crews mixed with theirs on the pier and we got to know some of them. One of the PT skippers we saw a lot of was named Kennedy. The guys said that I should go up and meet him, maybe he was a relative. I didn't go, of course, because enlisted men don't just go up to officers and introduce themselves. Besides, my relatives came from Tennessee; this lieutenant, Jack Kennedy, was from Massachusetts.

*   *   *

Two memorable things happened to me on Tulagi (and followed me on to Guadalcanal) — neither of which had to do with combat. First, a bunch of us popped out with a rash, a bad rash that started between the fingers then over the hands. It then broke out in the armpits, and lastly the groin area — and it itched the most maddening itch you can imagine. The fingers and hands itched the worst. Scratching made it worse, and made it bleed. It was so bad that we couldn't work and we couldn't sleep. Doc took a couple of guys over to the base sick bay, but the medics there didn't know what it was nor how to treat it so they called it "jungle rot" and painted the afflicted areas with potassium permanganate. We did look funny with our purple hands, feet, armpits, and genitals. The treatment didn't seem to help, but the medics didn't know what else to do. After a while, the tiny blisters slowly dried up — but they did come back periodically. This turned out to be a common affliction among the troops fighting in the Southwest Pacific; everyone, almost without exception, popped up with jungle rot on one or more parts of his anatomy.

The other thing that hit us was diagnosed as "dengue fever." It hit the first week we were on the island. Again, here was a jungle malady that the Americans knew little or nothing about. No one knew what caused it nor how to treat it. The locals called it "bone-break fever" — and that describes it very well. One morning one of the men said he didn't feel well, but he went out on the boat anyway. He was so ill by noon that he had to be carried to the main sick bay on a stretcher, as he screamed every step of the way from the pain inflicted by the motion. He was back on base in three days, weak as a kitten, but couldn't return to duty for another week. Sick bay had so many brought in from the various units that they wouldn't take the next victim from our outfit, said to keep him in bed and force fluids. I've never seen a person suffer like that — before or since. Just about everybody had it at least once before we left the islands. My turn came as I had that "funny feeling" when reveille sounded one morning — and by 1000 I was sick — sicker than I have ever been in my life. I was sent to bed and as I lay there, I took inventory of what was happening to my body: Every single muscle ached with so deep a pain that it felt like it started in the marrow of my bones. I lay very still because even the slightest motion meant excruciating pain. And strangely enough, it affected even the eye muscles. Not knowing this, when I wanted to look toward the porch, I cut my eyes to the left rather than face the pain of moving my head, and screamed with the unexpected pain from my eyeballs.

Doc came around often, even though there was nothing he could do. He couldn't even bathe my forehead with cool water because just a light touch was agonizing. He knew how I felt because he had been down with it too. Still, I appreciated his coming by just to speak to me.

"You okay, Kennedy?"

I wasn't, but I'd still murmur, "Yeah."

When all the guys got called out that afternoon on some emergency, I was alone for several hours. Before they left, Doc came by and slipped a morphine Syrette in my hand.

"I meant to give you a shot this afternoon. Keep this, and when you think you can't stand another minute of it, jab this in your hip and squeeze."

That last minute came a couple of hours later. There was

nobody in the area when I picked up the Syrette from the edge of the bunk where Doc had left it, and I screamed out loud with the wave of agony that coursed through my whole body from the simple motion of loosening the cap and jabbing the needle in my arm; it hurt too much trying to reach my backside. It took about 30 seconds for that blessed, blessed relief, so I lay there quietly and reveled in the newfound peace and comfort. I don't know what strength the morphine was, but I was pain-free for about an hour before it began reasserting itself but even then it wasn't as bad before. Doc gave me two sleeping pills that night; when I awoke the next morning, the pain was gone but I was so weak I had to have help getting to the latrine. I thought I had to urinate, but my body was so dehydrated from the fever that all I did was piddle a little air (it seemed).

*   *   *

As life became more and more peaceful on Tulagi, it got tougher and tougher on Guadalcanal, so we weren't surprised when orders came to join the Naval Operating Base on Guadalcanal at Kukum Beach.

Solomon Islands:
Second Stop

Point of information: In any war, only the Big Brass know what's going on. The men in the field do only what they are told to do. They are not told what will follow their immediate objective nor are they given any historic or strategic background on the campaign fought or duty performed. The battle(s) for the Solomon Islands was no exception. In retrospect, after reading some of the histories of the war in the Southwest Pacific these many years after it was over, I have a much better understanding of decisions, events, and strategies as they affected me.

Richard Tregaskis, in his *Guadalcanal Diary,* quotes a Marine saying, "What the hell we want to take some little place nobody ever heard of that we can't even pronounce its name?"

The Navy planners (Admirals King, Nimitz, et al.) agreed that it was time to stop the Japanese advance in the Pacific. In the eight months since the war started, the Japanese had slowly occupied just about everything in the Pacific from the Aleutian Islands in the north to the Solomon Islands in the south. If they were not stopped in the Solomons — where an airfield was now almost complete — they could go on, unchecked, to occupy New Hebrides and New Caledonia, and virtually cut all of America's supply line to Australia. If that happened, both Australia and New Zealand would fall without much of a fight. In the early planning phase, the Solomons invasion was supposed to be somewhat of a "hit and run" action, to slow the Japanese advance until the Brass thought of something more constructive to do. It never occurred to them until much later that this would be the first stepping stone to what would ultimately lead the United States all the way to Tokyo.

Britain and Australia governed most of the islands in the Southwest Pacific by mandate from the League of Nations after World War I. Australia did set up a series of "coastwatchers" along its own coastline to report any unusual or suspicious shipping activity, weather changes, etc. By 1940, the coastwatchers had reported so much suspicious activity by the Japanese maritime and naval ships in Australian waters that the Aussies decided to expand the Coastwatch System throughout its island protectorate. They were joined in this endeavor by the British. After the Japanese occupation of the islands, the British and Australian copra plantation managers (who constituted the majority of the watchers) were not yet endangered by the Japanese, but those who felt they were proceeded to abandon their plantations. Having nowhere to go and no way to get there, they took what provisions and "comforts of home" they could transport and hid out in the hills (or the "bush" as they called it), thus becoming full-time, clandestine coastwatchers. Their code name was "Ferdinand," after a Walt Disney comic character, Ferdinand the Bull; he didn't want to fight, all he wanted to do was smell the flowers! Unlike the Disney character, these Ferdinands were ready and willing to fight, but they were far more valuable to the Allied war effort by keeping tabs on the Japs.

All the Ferdinands had numerous hiding places throughout their territories, and they were equipped with provisions and radios. Actually, they had strict orders not to fight, but to run; their radios were a very valuable intelligence tool. Even though the Americans had broken the Japanese code, it was a coastwatcher who warned the British officials at Tulagi of their impending occupation — and it was also a coastwatcher who reported the construction of an airfield on Guadalcanal. The first air attack by the Japanese on the now-occupied Guadalcanal came the morning of the invasion; a watcher on Bouganville (350 miles away) reported a flight of bombers on the way to the island. By the time they arrived, the Navy transports were at sea and Marine fighter planes were airborne and waiting for them.

In the weeks before the first of August, the Brass had to move quickly before the Japanese made the airfield operational. Once completed, it would have been a base from which to launch bomb attacks on the New Hebrides and New Caledonia to the south, and even Fiji and Samoa to the east. In Allied hands, however, the airfield would be a base from which the Americans could bomb Japanese holdings at Rabual and New Guinea — and other enemy installations all the way to Japan.

*   *   *

It is not my intent to write a history of the battles in and around the Solomons, but one sea battle in particular, the night of August

8th and August 9th, is crucial in the fight for these particular islands. More Americans were killed in that one action than all the casualties suffered by our forces in six months of combat on the islands of Guadalcanal and Tulagi. The night of August 8th was a tragedy of errors: On that night, Admiral Turner (commander of the Allied amphibious force) notified General Vandergriff (commandant of the First Marines) and Admiral Crutchley (Australian commander of the Allied escort force) that all of the American aircraft carriers had pulled back to be refueled and rearmed, and that he (Admiral Turner) was pulling the transport ships out also because there was no air cover from the carriers. General Vandergriff had a fit, and rightly so, because over a thousand of his Marines had not yet been landed and more than half of his supplies (including food, ammo, artillery, and other critically needed supplies to complete construction of the airfield) were still aboard the transports. Admiral Turner did give General Vandergriff until dawn to get what he could off the transports.

Admiral Crutchley had failed to notify his ships of the line — cruisers, destroyers, frigates and assorted other warships — that he was pulling back 25 miles for the conference with Admiral Turner. As such, the ships under his command had no contact with their commander and they had no contact with each other; strict radio silence had been ordered! Even though the conference with Admiral Turner and General Vandergriff was concluded before midnight, Admiral Crutchley, for some unknown reason, chose not to rejoin his battle group. (Apparently, they did not even know he was gone.) Some time before dawn, with Admiral Crutchley some 25 miles away, the Japanese 8th Fleet came steaming up The Slot (Ironbottom Sound, the passage between Guadalcanal and Tulagi), undetected until they were within easy range of the Allied warships; their guns were primed and ready to fire. Finally, it was the destroyer USS *Blue* that sounded the alarm — but it was too late because the Japanese guns and torpedoes were already trained on the Allied fleet. Some of the ships were hit by torpedoes and shells as they were sounding the General Quarters alarm. It was a rout (a slaughter, actually) because the "protecting" Allied fleet had no commander and no communication with each other. The Battle of Savo Island lasted only forty minutes. The result: The Japanese force sank two cruisers and one destroyer, two cruisers were so badly damaged that they were later abandoned, and one cruiser had its entire bow blown off. The dead numbered 1,023, more than all the men who were killed in the six months of fighting it took to secure the islands of Guadalcanal and Tulagi. Another 800 men were wounded.

Another amazing thing happened: The Japanese fleet did not take the time to sink the loaded and defenseless American transport ships sitting there being offloaded; Admiral Mikawa's battle group did not know that the carriers were gone, so they were in a hurry to flee the scene before daylight, in hopes that their fleet would be out of range of the planes from the aircraft carriers. Had they sunk the transports, the Solomon Islands might well have returned to Japanese hands.

*   *   *

Back on Tulagi, we packed our bags and loaded them and the equipment from our machine shop, armory, ship's store, etc., on the lighters and were ready by midmorning to make the 20-mile crossing to Guadalcanal. But just before we were to board, several canoe loads of noisy natives from the island of Florida arrived with great fanfare: They had two Japanese prisoners, all tied up and pretty well beaten up. They could have been soldiers who had escaped from Tanambogo and Gavutu or they could have been the crew of a plane shot down on a bombing run. Whatever, the natives made us understand that they had been caught stealing chickens! One helluva fight must have ensued because the Japs were battered, bleeding, and bruised. No bones seemed to have been broken, but the bigger of the Japs had a right ear that had been torn very badly. In the fight over the chickens, the only way the Jap could be subdued was when a native was able to get a mouthful of ear.

Nobody wanted to transport the prisoners, so we loaded one on my boat and the other on the skipper's boat and headed for Guadalcanal. I had the big one with the chewed-up ear. We tried talking to him (hand signs and pidgin English) and believe we could have communicated, but he got seasick, real sick, and spent most of the 20 miles with his head over the side.

Our arrival on Kukum Beach was September 5, 1942. First thing we did was to turn our prisoners over to the Marines, then find a place to pitch our tents and unload the gear. We were surprised to learn that the beachmaster and sailors at the operating base were not Navy; they were Coast Guard. They were the guys who manned the boats loaded with Marines for the initial landing assault. Although we were now a part of that base, we operated independently, and we all worked our buns off.

Guadalcanal

From the very beginning, life on Guadalcanal was pure, unadulterated hell; Tulagi, on the other hand, was choice duty by comparison. Approaching Guadalcanal, we saw white sand and then beyond the gentle swaying of coconut palms, many of which were topless, their fronds having been blown off during the bombing and shelling. After the Marines had taken the prisoners away, we opened C rations and ate them, unheated, for lunch—a lunch that was a battle in itself because swarms of big black and green flies were everywhere. They immediately attacked the food in and on the can, on the spoon, and even on and in our mouths! It was not unusual for someone to spit out a mouthful of food because a fly had gone in with it. First few times, someone would vomit, then we got as used to it as we could. I wonder how many big black and green flies I've eaten, unknowingly?

Many movie-like things happened to us on Guadalcanal, things that I remember very well, such as the bombings and shellings we survived, the landings we made up and down the beach with Marine raiding parties, and the shooting at the Jap bombers and fighters when they flew over us at 100 feet. What I remember even more vividly are the day-to-day hellish things that are never even alluded to in the movies, but are in a few of the history books. They never sound so bad as the actual experience. For instance, the remembrance of the flies still makes me shudder. They were more repulsive, I guess, because we knew that they came from the maggots that fed on the dead Jap soldiers. The medics said that was why the diarrhea and dysentery was so severe. I do believe that every single sailor and Marine on that island had diarrhea all the time to one degree or another: You either had it or you had it *bad!* The first time or two someone messed his drawers, we kidded him and gave him a bad time. Kinda funny. It wasn't very long before that kind of kidding stopped, though, because it eventually happened to each of us and it's no fun to be the butt of your own joke.

After dark, the mosquitoes came out in great swarms. Some guys had mosquito nets that fitted over their helmets and were tied around their necks. They were safe from attack if their sleeves were rolled down and their hands were in their pockets. Mosquito netting over our cots was a must. There was no way you could sleep at night without one. The trick was to get inside it without letting mosquitoes in with you. I sometimes slept with my arm over my head, where it rested against the mosquito net — and the next morning my arm would be chewed up and swollen from the hundreds of bites through the netting. We were supposed to have had quinine capsules very day but the quinine was shipped in bulk, as were the capsules. The medics were supposed to have filled the capsules, but the heat and humidity fused the gelatin capsules into one big blob. We tried taking quinine by spoon with a water chaser. Yecht! It was so bitter that those who didn't spit it up threw it up; however, it was something we had to have. Many, not realizing the consequences, gave it up. Others of us would roll it in toilet paper or cigarette paper, then try to swallow it fast before the paper got soaked with saliva and disintegrated. It worked sometimes. I read a statistic somewhere that 90 percent of the troops on the island came down with a malaria attack at least once during a tour of duty there. It was not a statistic that I was happy to be a part of.

After two or three months, a new drug, Atabrine, replaced quinine as a malaria preventive, but the Marines wouldn't take it (and some sailors too); the scuttlebutt got all over the island that Atabrine made a man impotent. As a consequence, malaria was so bad at one point that medics stood at the end of the chow line and actually placed the pill on the tongue of each Marine going through. I'm told that some men would slip the pill under his tongue, then spit it out a few steps on down the line.

*　　　*　　　*

Another of the unpleasant things I remember about the war was "Washing Machine Charlie" — a single-engine Jap airplane that would fly back and forth over the 3 × 5-mile strip of the part of the island that the Americans occupied. Every 20 to 30 minutes throughout the night, he would drop an antipersonnel bomb somewhere; other times, he dropped bottles or something that whistled like bombs as they fell to the earth; it made us cringe, waiting for the explosion that never came. Charlie's primary purpose was not to kill people; he was out to destroy morale. After backbreaking work all day long, and being hungry, we needed our rest, and we couldn't get it in a foxhole that was swarming with mosquitoes and smelling of stale sweat and urine. After a while, we wouldn't get out of bed when Washing Machine Charlie came over, knowing that the bomb or two he would drop probably wouldn't hit anywhere near where we were. We didn't, that is, until the night one of his random little bombs hit a tent near us, right square in the middle where eight Marines were sleeping. We saw their bodies — or what was left of their bodies; there was hardly enough left to bury. From that point on, we spent our nights in the foxholes with the mosquitoes and foul odors while Charlie was doing his thing.

*   *   *

Our foxholes were dug to accommodate one tent: eight men. We had to displace one helluva lot of sand since the sides kept caving in. When we had the right width and length, we would shore up the sides and cover the top with coconut logs, then pile bags of sand at least a couple of feet thick on top of the logs. There was an entrance or passageway at each end. As you can imagine, there was very little ventilation, so the air got ripe very quickly — and it was all compounded by swarms of mosquitoes that were thick enough to cut with a knife. But there was sometimes brightness in the midst of misery — in the form of a sometime pet.

Tojo

We had a dog, a pet, that belonged to all 19,000 Marines and sailors. His name was "Tojo," the most intelligent and unusual animal I have ever seen.

Tojo was a big white mongrel—a pup less than a year old when the Marines landed. No one knows where he came from but we do know he was no loyal friend of the Japs. The Japs hid out in the bush when the Marines landed, but Tojo stayed behind and became the friend and mascot of the American invasion force. Not just one unit, *all* of them. Unlike most domestic pets, Tojo had no favorites; he was in and around every unit, was fed wherever he was when he made it obvious he was hungry (even when we were on short rations Tojo ate better than we did), and he would play and frolic with anyone who had time for him—and we usually took the time.

Tojo didn't like bombs and shells and headed for the nearest foxhole when he saw us running. After a little while, he learned the meaning of the siren that sounded General Quarters when enemy planes were approaching; he would race to shelter at the first wail, usually getting inside before we did. When the bombs or shells hit, he would nuzzle up and whine to whomever he happened to be with in the hole. When the "all clear" sounded, he was the first one out, running and frolicking as though nothing had happened.

Each unit felt that Tojo belonged, personally, to them, because when he was with them, he was theirs completely. He would show up suddenly in our area (or any area, for that matter) and act as though he owned the place. We fed him and played with him and he, in return, gave us his undivided attention and affection. About the time we thought we had won him over and he was ours for keeps, that fickle dog would take off and give his loyalties to another outfit, sometimes a mile away. But we were always his grateful mistress; we were glad to see him when he came back. His last desertion was forgiven and we vied for his affection. We could blot the reality of all unpleasantness when we threw a coconut for Tojo to retrieve and laughed as we watched him work to get a grip on the slick surface, which he always managed to do.

The Maladies of War

The old jungle rot was constant; someone was painted most of the time with the potassium permanganate — and out of the 60 men in our section, there were usually two or three down with dengue or malaria. As the malaria started to hit us, we could have as many as 20 men down at a time. Funny thing about malaria, it comes on so suddenly. One day I went to chow, but when I sat down to eat, I couldn't — no appetite. I couldn't work the boat, so Doc took me by the arm and led me to the main sick bay, very close to our tent area. Doc didn't say a word, but the medic on duty looked at me and said, "Put him on the cot over there."

Doc left and I lay there feeling worse and worse and getting colder and colder. When I called for help, someone brought me another blanket or two. Within half an hour, I was shivering uncontrollably and I couldn't keep my teeth from chattering.

"Please give me something."

"Sorry, Mac, there ain't nothing that will help you except some Atabrine after your fever breaks."

They took my temperature every half hour. I thought I was dying when it hit 105 degrees; I was so sick that the thought of death was a welcome one, but this wasn't the time because the temperature went higher and I passed out. I had several attacks after that and I remember that I always prayed that God would get the fever up real fast so that I would be knocked unconscious and oblivious to the pain. Attacks always leave the patient helpless for at least a couple of days; it takes that long to get the fluids back in the system and food enough to get a little strength back.

*   *   *

Anyone approaching Kukum Beach — or anywhere along the coastline that fronted a grove of coconut trees — would think that Guadalcanal was a tropical paradise. As we approached the beach that day coming over from Tulagi, I thought of another popular song that was on the Lucky Strike Hit Parade; it started like this, "A sleepy lagoon, a tropical moon, and you on an island...."

It looked like a place which was going to be everything we expected of that island in the song: A lush green mountain in the
distance, untouched by civilization, etc. And everything was lovely
on the beach, but once you step out of the coconut grove into the
bush, *watch out!* Everything is soggy and wet in the jungle because
it rains so much. I saw one area from a distance that was covered
with beautiful, swaying grass, but the distance made it deceptive. Up
close, it was grass all right, kunia grass, six feet tall with edges like
hacksaw blades that cut the Marines to pieces when they tried going
through it. I don't have the words to describe how bad it was, but
a Marine machine gunner named Robert Leckie kept a meticulous
account of the island and his experiences there. This is how he
described what lay beneath the exterior beauty: "she was a mass of
slops and stinks and pestilence; of scum-crested lagoons and vile
swamp inhabited by giant crocodiles; a place of spiders as big as
your fist and wasps and long as your finger, of lizards ... tree
leeches ... scorpions ... centipedes whose foul scurrying across
human skin leaves a track of inflamed flesh... By night, mosquitoes
come in clouds — bringing malaria, dengue or any one of a dozen
filthy exotic fevers... And Guadalcanal stank. She was sour with
the odor of her own decay, her breath so hot and humid, so sullen
and so still, that the Marines cursed and swore to feel the vitality
oozing from them in a steady stream of enervating sweat...."

Amen. As Walter Cronkite was to say, "and that's the way it
was...."

*   *   *

The food was another vivid memory. On Tulagi, it was no
problem because of the vast stores of Japanese supplies left behind.
Too, we still had supplies from the cargo ship the Japs were shooting
at the night we arrived — but food was a problem in that campaign,
off and on, for months. The initial landings involved 19,000 troops
(16,000 Marines plus a 3,000-man ancillary force of naval shore
operations). Our supply ships came in sporadically because in the
beginning the Japanese dominated both sea and air much (if not
most) of the time. It seemed that we were constantly on "short rations" — which meant two skimpy meals per day — sometimes less.
When our supplies ran out, the cooks resorted to the storehouses
piled high with bags of Japanese rice. Weevils were in it, of course,
but the galley hands did a pretty good job of picking them out before
they were cooked. Those they missed, we found and flipped out.

After a while, though, we just didn't give a damn. What the hell, it's only enriched with a little protein. We ate without even looking down. And the flies, those damnable flies, they were always there.

*   *   *

The mail delivery service, oddly enough, was pretty good—two to three weeks for mail, each way, if the "V-Mail" single-sheet stationery was used. The mail would go to a central spot in the States to be photostated, then a small roll of photostated film would be sent to a place in our area to be printed, then delivered to the troops.

A few days before we left Tiburon, California, my mother had baked a jam cake (one of my favorites) and mailed it to me; I didn't receive it in California, of course, and didn't expect to receive it at all. Much to my surprise, I received a package at mail call in October. Sure enough, there was the jam cake—and in remarkably good condition after four months in transit. It was pretty badly broken up from the long trip and rough handling, but it was edible—a little bit dry, but really not bad.

The cake was on a dinner plate from a set that my folks had bought from the Jewel Tea Company; it was yellow with brown flowers around the rim. From that day on, I had all my meals on that plate. It was really something to go through a chow line where the mess cooks threw gobs of whatever was called food that day in our mess kits—but there I was, gently holding out my dinner plate. I'm convinced being served that way made the food taste better.

Those first few months were pretty tough because of the shortages; we seemed to be short of everything—everything but ammunition. We heard all the scuttlebutt and the bitching about what was going on and what we were short of, but I never heard of an ammunition shortage. If any shortage prevailed, it was food—and when food is in short supply, then the troops are put on what has always been called "short rations" in the Navy. Short rations, to us, meant something like a small serving of powdered eggs, hardtack, a little jam if we had it, and coffee (there was never a shortage of coffee) for breakfast. Lunch was hardtack and coffee, and dinner was Spam, hardtack, and coffee.

There would be slight variations, but by and large, that was it. All small servings, of course. In fact, we were on short rations so long that the first of a "regular" meal would give most of us more diarrhea. For some unexplained reason, the Navy rarely ever got C rations, so the Marines in the field usually ate better than we did at the Operating Base.

And the Wind Blew...

Because of the flies — which the medics were convinced carried dengue fever as well as dysentery, adequate sanitary facilities were a must. A huge hole was dug for garbage disposal. This hole was topped with a roof and screen siding. When it was full, we covered it with sand, dug another hole, and moved the old covering over the new hole. The same applied to the latrine. Most of the men used the great outdoors, behind a tree away from the tents, to urinate. For the other necessity, we had a four-holer. It, too, was roofed and had screen sidings, but the four-holer was mounted on a wooden deck platform that was placed over a huge hole in the sand. And it didn't take 60 men very long to fill it.

When this happened the first time, four of us who had extra duty to work off were told to cover the hole, dig another, and place the old platform and cover the new hole. Digging a latrine was much like digging a foxhole; with the sand continually caving in, we had to dig a hole twice to three times as large as what we actually wanted, then shore up the sides to the proper dimensions. We came up with a collective, labor-saving idea; we found a way we thought was better and easier than the back-breaking job of digging. Why didn't we just move the cover and decking, then fill the hole with Japanese gasoline that was cached not far from our dig. We thought that a 55-gallon drum would be enough to incinerate the waste, then all we would have to do was put the platform and cover back over the old hole. Well, we got the gasoline, two drums of what we later learned was aviation gasoline. The Jap gasoline was worthless because it couldn't be used in our planes as the octane was not high enough, and the octane was too high to be used in jeeps and trucks.

After we had moved the platform, we dumped not one but two drums of gasoline — 110 gallons — in that hole. The stuff in the hole was actually floating in gasoline for a few moments before it was absorbed into the sand. One of us (I don't remember who) got a hand grenade, and from a safe distance behind a tree lobbed it into the hole to start the fire. Problem was, it didn't start a fire, *it caused an explosion!* And when it blew, it carried everything in that hole more than 100 feet into the air and scattered the burning contents in a wide radius that covered (and I do mean covered) our living quarters, kitchen, sick bay, etc. I don't know whether we coined the little ditty that was sung around camp after that, but the words did fit:

> "The wind blew
> and the shit flew
> and we couldn't see
> for a minute or two."

And we saw the first mushroom cloud of the war, but this one was filled with other than radioactive material!

Another Captain's Mast, another butt-chewing, more extra duty, and we had to retrieve *every single piece* of the contents from that hole!

"The miseries of war...."

Shootin' the Breeze

I didn't think much about it at the time, but a lot of the discussion that took place when things were really tough was about, of all things, boot camp! In our unit, there were very few of us who had been to the same boot camp—and whoever was telling the story, his was the toughest, or easiest, or best, or worst boot camp ever. This was not only true of the sailors but also of the Marines we worked with on the boats when we were unloading cargo.

Before the beachmaster had us arrested, there was one memorable discussion of what was taught at the Marine boot camp in San Diego. It took place while the boat was laying off from a freighter, waiting to go in for another load of aviation gasoline in 55-gallon drums. It was a pretty long wait, so we broke out a case of peaches that we had stowed in the stern sheets and opened a gallon can with a bayonet. It was like receiving from the common cup; we passed it from person to person, each eating a peach or two then passing it on to the next guy. And as we ate, we talked, sometimes to the group, sometimes to just the next guy.

The discussion started when two Marines began talking about the merits of various kinds of meat that were not the normal bill of fare: rattlesnake, possum, and horse. The group didn't join in on this scintillating conversation, or even act interested in it, until the remarks were made about the military serving this kind of meat. Nobody in the boat would eat rattlesnake or possum, but there were varying degrees of prejudice about eating horse meat, the consensus being that it was clean and couldn't be a lot different from eating veal (which we believed was an unborn bovine fetus). Veal, horse, it was all clean, so the topic died quietly with a story about the Marines eating horse meat at boot camp at Parris Island, South Carolina.

Seems that roast horse, unbeknownst to the troops, was being served at evening chow. About 15 minutes into the meal, a sergeant stepped into the chow hall to make an announcement and almost collided with a kid doing KP who was running to the kitchen with a load of dirty dishes. The sergeant yelled to him, "Whoa."

And within three minutes, 14 Marines had choked to death.

* * *

The conversation moved on, somehow, to the Marine's most treasured possession: his rifle. The drill instructors in boot camp pounded into the new recruits the value of his weapon and saw to it that they treated it as tenderly and lovingly as if it were an only child. If it was not clean enough at inspection, and especially if he ever dropped it, punishment was his having to sleep with the rifle a given number of nights. After all, a rifle was the Marine's best friend. It had three functions: You could shoot it, you could affix a bayonet to it and use it as a spear, and you could grasp it by the barrel and swing it like a club. Three most important uses that were all life-protecting.

The topic then swung to the Marine's next most important possession: the helmet. No instruction was given in boot camp about the helmet except how to wear it—nothing about its many other uses. The Marines in combat in the Solomons learned the hard way about how valuable and how utilitarian a tool his helmet really was. At this point, all six guys in the boat had joined the discussion, and most made a worthy contribution.

First, a helmet could save your life; you wore it to deflect (hopefully) a bullet or a piece of shrapnel. One Marine had even proved that a helmet would stop a 45-caliber slug fired from 25 feet. (The crushed but unpenetrated helmet would have killed the Marine, but it did withstand the force of the slug.)

Second, a helmet could be used as a cook pot. One one occasion, a squad of enterprising Marines who were sick of eating cold C rations in the field each emptied his C ration tin of meat into one helmet (with the liner removed) where it was then placed over a fire to heat. It worked so well that this ploy was later taught to all recruits.

Third, it could serve as a wash basin for personal hygiene. Stripped to the waist, a Marine could get a pretty good spit bath with one helmet full of cold water and a little soap. It was even better if he put the helmet over a fire and heated the water. And the hot water made the shaving a whole lot easier.

Fourth, it was an ideal wash pot for small articles of clothing such as socks, underwear, etc.

Fifth, and by no means last, the helmet could be used as a potty—and it was, on occasion. When acute and chronic diarrhea strikes, it has no respect for time and circumstance; if the cramp in the gut hits while the shells are whistling in or the bombs are falling, nature most always prevails. (Actually, a screaming shell or a whis-tling bomb has been known to hasten the action.) What to do? There's really not much choice. Next to the worst thing a guy could do was mess his drawers; the worst thing was to go outside and get his arse blown off. And one of the more socially unacceptable things was mess on the floor of the foxhole. It just wasn't done, not in our newly created social order. Nobody said anything if you quietly slipped out the liner and then squatted over your helmet in the L-shaped entry of the foxhole in answer to nature's call. It gave a feel-ing of semi-privacy at least.

"Sorry, fellas."

"That's okay."

During the months that followed, I heard of many more uses for the helmet, but nothing original; everything fitted into one of the five categories discussed.

Henderson Field

Although Henderson Field was less than a mile from our operating base, I went there only twice during the months we served on the island—and both times were eye-openers because things there were beyond our wildest expectations.

A Marine engineering battalion finished up the work left undone by the Jap labor battalion—and they did it in less than two weeks. All of their construction equipment was still on the transports that Admiral Turner ordered out of the area when the Japanese Eighth Fleet sank everything in sight the morning of August 9th. Very little of their equipment and supplies were needed to complete the job on the airfield because the Japanese had left them everything they needed—and they left it in a very orderly fashion.

The Allies knew that the airfield was not operational, so did not bomb or shell that area; they concentrated on the beaches and the inland areas where the enemy was more likely to be dug in. When the engineers reached the airfield they found slight damage, and everything there could be utilized: There were over 100 Ford-type trucks and other vehicles in perfect operating condition complete with big stores of parts, gasoline and oil, bulldozers, well-equipped machine shops, tool sheds, tons of cement, dynamite and blasting caps—*everything* needed to complete the field. There was also a dispensary where our medics found surgical instruments far superior to anything they had ever seen in the States. And to top it off, there was a large multi-room structure that served as a headquarters unit and officers billet. When I saw it, the Marines were using it for recreation and billets. Over the door was a hastily painted sign that said "Tokyo Hilton" or some such popular name. There was also a commercial icemaking machine. Over the door of the building that housed it was another hand-lettered sign saying:

TOJO ICE FACTORY
Under New Management

Once operational, the airfield became the home base for at least a couple of fighter squadrons, and probably more. It was operational but a lot of work was still going on. The engineers were lengthening and widening the field so that the big Air Corps B-17 bombers could take off and land from there.

One more thing the engineers found: When the Jap bomber formations flew over to bomb the field, the Marines took cover in the foxholes that the Japs had made to be used when the Americans flew over to bomb them!

My next and last trip to Henderson Field was after Christmas — probably January of 1943. The field was then huge compared to what I had seen before. There were perhaps a hundred of all kinds of planes — fighters, amphibs, scout, bombers, *everything*. There were also many lean-to type buildings with thatched roofs that had been built with the help of the curious natives who had come in from the bush. They were leery of white American outsiders at first because the Japs, also outsiders, had mistreated them. In a short time they came to like the Americans, and it wasn't long before most had a limited English vocabulary: "Cigarette?" "Candy me bebe?"

And, of course, they got 'em.

*   *   *

On the last trip to Henderson, I stopped in Personnel and talked to the chief yeoman. I told him my story about the Cadet Selection Board and asked if he would help me follow through on it.

"Listen, Mac," he said, "there is nothing that can be done in this office. Your best bet is to go through your own commanding officer, and if that doesn't work, go to the first Naval Air Station you come to outside the combat zone."

If I went to my own CO again, he'd kill me — if the chief yeoman didn't do it first.

The River

One of the major problems that followed the Marine Corps in this campaign was that of personal hygiene. For the first five of the six months the Marines battled the Japs on Guadalcanal, the Marines were on the defensive, dug in on the perimeter that surrounded our little piece of the island. For days and weeks at a time, they lived on the line in dugouts, foxholes, and any other place they thought would keep them from getting shot. And they slept in their clothing. The only fresh water they could rely on was what they carried in their canteens. They were lucky to have enough to shave with and to brush their teeth regularly. Baths and clean clothing would be waiting back at the base camp, once their relief came. Until they got back to the relative comfort and cleanliness of eight-man tents pitched in the coconut groves near the beach, they had to suffer with myriads of mosquitoes, body lice, coconut crabs, rats, and jungle rot between toes, fingers, in and around the crotch, and armpits down to the elbows. And life on and off the line was one constant trip to or from the latrine with an anus too tender to touch with a powderpuff.

The sailors on the beach, bless our hearts, missed many of the physical discomforts that went with Marine duty on the line or on patrol. For one thing, there was never a sailor, Navy or Coast Guard, who had body lice. At least none that I knew of. The difference between having them and not having them is *water;* the sailors were on the boats almost every day, and taking a swim in the ocean was a usual part of working on water craft. Without a freshwater shower afterward, the skin was a little sticky for a while, but it was sure better than being dirty—and I suppose it drowned the nits that were sure to grow into lice.

* * *

There was one favorite spot on the Tenaru River where sailors and Marines gathered for a common ritual—washing their bodies and washing their clothes. There were two bridges the engineers had built over the Tenaru; one was a low bridge, 400 or 500 feet across which spanned a depth of perhaps three or four feet of water. There was another bridge about a quarter of a mile upstream, a tall one whose span was a good 50 feet above the water. Both bridges had an impact on my life during the months I spent on that island. One good, one not so good.

*   *   *

About 50 feet upriver from the lower bridge, a giant tree had fallen many years before and was lodged on a sandbar in the center of and parallel to the river. It was a huge tree, perhaps 125 feet tall and a good four feet in diameter. It lay there with half its trunk above the water, a perfect place for a man to stand and scrub his dirty clothes on the smooth surface of the exposed old wood.

Standing by that fallen tree with the water almost to my waist is one of my fond memories of the war. I made it to the river every week or ten days—or more often if I ran out of clean clothes and could finagle a little extra time off. The ritual followed by the sailors and Marines who congregated there was always the same. First, frolic in the water for a while and use half a bar of soap in an effort to wash the jungle stink off the body, then find a spot at the log to belly up to and wash dirty laundry. Sailors and Marines were issued a scrub brush in boot camp, a little wooden job about eight inches long with multiple rows of the toughest bristles I have ever seen. When they were issued, we were told that they were guaranteed to last a 20-year enlistment. And I believe they were that good.

On two different occasions, I happened to be at the scrub log doing my laundry a day or so after the Marines and Japs had had a battle somewhere upstream. We saw part of the results when the bodies of Jap soldiers would float downstream on their way to the ocean, always face down and bloated. They resembled overstuffed dolls. A detail downstream would retrieve the bodies and see that they were buried. Dead Marines would sometimes float down. When they did, we would pull them up on the river bank then send a runner to notify the nearest headquarters company.

On one of my weekly excursions, while I was scrubbing on a pair of dirty pants, a detail of Marines were coming off patrol, crossing the bridge on their way back to their base camp. One of them stopped and yelled toward the log, "Hey, Kennedy!"

Don't know where their patrol had been, but they were all covered with filth and whiskers. One Marine looked pretty much like another, so I swam up to the bridge to see who had called me. Much to my surprise and pleasure, there stood a kid I was in high school with. As his squad was crossing the bridge, he looked down and saw a pile of neatly folded dungarees with the name Bill Kennedy stenciled on the shirt. We knew each other real well back in Lubbock but were not close friends; nevertheless, it was great to see a familar face. His sergeant gave him 15 minutes off, so we stood there in the water up to our waists, me naked and him fully clothed in combat gear, and talked about home.

*   *   *

About mid–November of 1943 was another time back at the log; just about everything I owned was dirty, so I quickly soaped down and rinsed off, then turned to the log. While we were all hard at work doing our laundry, a voice from the bridge called out to us.

"Hey, fellas, look over this way."

Didn't recognize the uniform; he was in khakis and wearing a pith helmet with no insignia on it — and he was pointing a camera at us. He was a war correspondent/photographer. Never did know his name. Scuttlebutt had it a day or so ago that a big shot from one of the wire services was on the island doing a story. We sure didn't expect to see anyone. When the big shots had come in before, military or correspondents, they stayed very close to headquarters and the officers' club, which was a big field hospital tent that had been pitched near the Tojo Ice Factory. The principal attraction there, we heard, was iced coffee and ice water — and Cokes when they were available. Being a shore station, they could have had beer and booze but General Vandergriff said no, not until the enlisted men could have the same privileges. He was that kind of leader. I'm sorry I never got to see the man who could lead his troops to hell and back.

Anyway, we smiled for the camera.

"Look, fellas, turn a little sideways. This is for *Life* magazine and they won't run it if any peckers are showing. Give it another try."

After a little more banter and five or six more shots, he said goodbye and good luck and took off for Henderson Field, walking and snapping pictures along the way. I dismissed the picture-taking incident until I received a letter from home a couple of months later. My sister sent a full page photograph out of *Life,* a picture of a bunch of naked GIs washing clothes on a big fallen log in the middle of the Tenaru River. It was tasteful; only the parts of some rear ends

Bathing and washing clothes in the Tenaru River. The author is the bather on the right holding a large dark towel. *Photo credit:* Ralph Morse, *Life Magazine* ©. Time Warner Inc.

were exposed. One GI was trying to cover his nakedness so as to not offend the sensitivities of the folks back home, so he had ducked down to grab a dungaree jacket to cover himself. When he did, his face was obscured by the shoulder of the guy in front. He was the only guy in the photograph whose family couldn't point and say, "That's my boy." That boy was me. Anyway, I did appear in a full-page photograph in a major national weekly magazine, but I'm the only one who knows it's me!

*   *   *

The other bridge, the tall one, could well have been the end of the war for me, my going home in a flag-covered pine box.

It happened this way: One of the supply dumps was a couple of miles away from our Operating Base; the dump was at the edge of the jungle in a small ravine recessed in between two big hummocks of earth. Good place for it because it was secure from three sides, which made pilfering almost impossible. The place was well-guarded by a detail of Marines.

We needed supplies of some kind, so the CO sent the newly promoted chief, a career ol' salt named Seaman—no pun intended—to take the requisition personally because it shortened the red tape involved. A hand-carried requisition could get results in a day or so; going through proper channels would take a week—if you were lucky.

"Take my jeep."

The CO's jeep was special. He didn't have enough rank to rate one when we first arrived there—and still didn't, for that matter. Nobody knew where he got the jeep but more than likely it was acquired by what was called a "midnight requisition." Mr. Carpenter wouldn't appreciate the term, "auto theft," so we have to assume that some unit had an excess number of jeeps, and that he simply "borrowed" one until they needed it back. He was proud of that jeep! Kept it washed, filled with gas, and ready to go at all times. If it had been a Cadillac back home in Los Angeles, he couldn't have been prouder of it. Even Chief Seaman was surprised when he said, "Take my jeep." How else are you going to show someone that you're a big shot if you're not magnanimous?

Seaman came out of the CO's tent and saw me standing nearby talking to Tony, our Greek cook.

"Kennedy, come go with me."

We walked over to the jeep and he handed me the keys.

"You drive."

The world is full of surprises. Seaman wanted to show me that he was a big shot too! And I was tickled to death that they were both egotistical because I hadn't driven a vehicle in months.

The drive over was nice; the sky was clear except for a few lazy-looking clouds that looked like they were trying to nuzzle up to Mount Austen in the distance. There were very few vehicles in the ruts we laughingly called a road. Even the Marines who manned the supply dump didn't give us a bad time, which they usually did. They were so hard to get along with most of the time, you'd think the supply dump belonged to them, personally. This time, though, they examined the chit, examined the authorization list, then checked the requisition against the inventory. Bingo!

"You got it, Chief. The truck oughta be over there with this stuff sometime this afternoon."

On the drive back — we were in no hurry — we saw a couple of Marines with big bundles swung over their shoulders, on their way to the river to do the laundry.

"Stop and give 'em a lift."

Everything was fine until we got to the bridge. Actually, it was fine until we got *on* the bridge. The bridge was built between two points of land that spanned a distance of a couple of hundred feet or so, and at any point on the bridge, we could look down at the river some 50 feet below. The bridge was just wide enough to accommodate a jeep or a small lightly loaded truck. Cross timbers covered the top of the span and 1″ × 10″ planks lay end to end as sort of a track for the vehicles to run on. The guard rail, if you could call it that, consisted of coconut logs laid end to end at the outer edge of the bridge, and ran the length of it on both sides. Fortunately, the logs were well anchored.

Traffic on the bridge was fairly heavy, so a lot of mud had accumulated on the surface; it was slick. I was only doing about 25 miles per hour but had to tap the brakes lightly to miss a coconut lying on one of the tread tracks. When the brakes caught, the rear end of the jeep fishtailed and slid off the tracks onto the crossties and broadside against the coconut guard rails. There the jeep continued to slide, its two right wheels against the coconut logs. We expected to go over the side any minute; the wheels would jump the guard rail or one of the coconut logs would give way — but neither happened. We made it all the way to the end of the bridge!

But it wasn't over yet. When the jeep reached the end of the bridge, the wheels rolled onto the apron that was a 15 degree slope down the side of the hill—which would have taken us all the way down to the bank of the river, to a cut that fell straight down, 15 feet to the water. I threw the jeep into low gear, cut the wheels sharply to the left, and gunned the engine, hoping to make it back to the road. It seemed like good strategy at the time, but when I cut the wheels left, the jeep rolled over to the right—and it rolled three times.

It was then that some of us should have earned the pine box, but not a single person was hurt—not even anything minor. As I was thrown from the jeep, I saw bodies flying everywhere. I remember thinking what a shameful thing it would be to get killed in a one-vehicle domestic-type auto accident in the middle of a war! I even visualized a telegram from the War Department saying something like,

"We regret to inform you that your dumb-ass son got himself killed in a one-vehicle accident that would never have happened if he had been a better driver.

/s/ Henry L. Stimpson.
Secretary of War"

Funny how thoughts rush through your head under the most unlikely circumstances—and this came to me as I was floating through the air just before I made an ungraceful landing squarely on my backside. When the jeep finally came to rest at the lip on the edge of the river—at the 15-foot drop point—I heard the Chief:

"Everybody okay?"

"Yeah."

"I think so."

"Yessir."

By this time, we had drawn a crowd. Don't know why one little accident of that kind would attract so much attention where we were, but bystanders always come to look. Chief Seaman, with his most authoritarian voice, ordered the onlookers to come give us a hand at turning the jeep right side up. When I stepped back to look, I wished that the damn thing had gone on over into the river. It was badly wrecked; it was *very* badly wrecked, but surprisingly, the engine ran and it was driveable.

The surprises for the day were not over. What was not surprising, though, was that our two Marine passengers decided to walk the rest of the way.

"It's no trouble, we'll be glad to take you on over."

"Thanks just the same; we'd just as soon walk."

Chief Seaman started on me the minute we drove off. (Strange that he let me get back behind the wheel.) Man, he was mad! He ranted and raved all the way back to Base and by the time we got there I was convinced that the Navy would deduct the cost of the jeep from my pay and that the CO would have me doing extra duty for the next 25 years. The surprise of the day came when the CO learned what happened. It was not *me* he was angry at; it was *Chief Seaman!* The CO didn't say a word to me, but he gave Seaman hell for letting me drive! I slipped quietly away while the ruckus was still going on. What was said remained personal between the CO and the Chief; nobody ever heard what was verbalized in there. I didn't quite escape that little episode unscathed, however. Every time there was a dirty detail, or a night watch, or something unpleasant or dangerous, guess who the chief called first?

"KENNEDY!"

"Coming, Chief."

"My head is bloody, but unbowed..."

Combat Duty

The chief function of the Naval Operating Base on Guadalcanal was to move Marines and supplies. By November of 1942, the first Marine Division (of which we were a part) was slowly being replaced by the second Marines and two Army infantry divisions, the 25th and the Americal—probably 30,000 to 35,000 men. However many, it was a bunch because we had to haul every single one of them, the replacements and those being replaced. We had to take the first Marines to the transports which would take them to New Zealand and Australia for R&R (Rest and Relaxation) before they went back into action on Tarawa, New Guinea, or to other places that we had never heard of. The rest of the time we spent running the empty boats to a ship, then running them back to shore when they were full. We always had Marine work parties that helped us with the heavy stuff.

We did all these things and we also maintained our own shops ashore such as the armory, sick bay, machine shops, warehouses, small stores, etc. Another job we had was hauling Marine raiding parties where they wanted to go. The Brass usually asked for volunteers, but it didn't matter because everybody always volunteered anyway.

Let me say here what very few people know about the initial landings in the Solomons: The U.S. Coast Guard, not the U.S. Navy, was tabbed for that job and once ashore, it was they who began putting the operating base together. Their beachmaster, and later ours, was a lieutenant named Deveraux. More on Mr. Deveraux later.

*   *   *

One day in October or November, a small group of us—three sailors and three Coast Guardsmen—were asked if we would volunteer to take an Englishman (a coastwatcher) about 20 miles down the coast to an area behind the Japanese lines. I feel sure that I was asked to go because I had the Browning automatic rifle and knew how to use it. Before we left the base, all six of us were armed

The author, hands on hips, watches Marines board for the trip to the transport in the background. *Photo credit:* Ralph Morse, *Life Magazine* ©. Time Warner Inc.

with a sidearm and had an automatic weapon as well. We never knew what the mission really was; we were never briefed on anything, it was simply a matter of following orders on a day by day basis. It must have been successful because the Coast Guardsmen were shortly thereafter awarded the Bronze Star for bravery or meritorious duty. We Navy sailors were told that we would get the same decoration, but never heard another word about it.

The mission itself was rather like a holiday until I came down again with another malaria attack. Before the fever, however, our mission was well under way. We went down the coast to a spot designated by Ferdinand, the coastwatcher. We dropped him off for the night, but before he left, he told us to go farther down the coast to a native village where we were to spend the night with the natives. We found this delightful village and were surprised that there were two priests there who taught at the school and ministered to the native tribe. Many of the older students were fluent in English — and they spoke it like Oxford scholars because that is where their teachers were educated! Had a good dinner that night and enjoyed entertainment provided by the younger children in the school. They sang songs for us, recited poetry, etc., just like young children back home do on "Home Room" night. We declined the priests' invitation to spend the night, so went offshore and anchored out of range from the mosquitoes — and the Japs, we hoped.

After breakfast the next morning, we returned for Ferdinand. While he was tending to business of some kind, he had us to sound an area of a cove nearby (that is, we measured the depth of the water in the cove).

Late that afternoon, he called us in. We went ashore to what had once been a beautiful plantation. Ferdinand's black companions from the bush took our rations and combined them with fresh local fruits and vegetables. It was quite a feast — and to this day, I do not know what some of the fruits were. Whatever we had, it was our first decent meal in months.

After dinner, Ferdinand (he never did tell us his name) told us that we would be sleeping in the house that night, and that before dawn we were to go about a mile inland to where a squad of Jap soldiers were spending the night; that we were to then eliminate (annihilate!) the entire squad. (That was Marine work, but when no one protested, the briefing continued; we were never told, but we always wondered why we had been selected for this job.) The natives would take care of the guard beforehand, if there was one. You can't imagine how excited I was at the thought of getting a Jap! It was almost as good as the thought of getting to be a cadet and learning to fly an airplane.

I missed out on this part of the operation. By 9 P.M. I knew I was on my way to malarialand, so the guys took me back to the boat, took it out a few hundred yards in the cove and anchored, then went back ashore in a canoe to rejoin the others in the house. My temperature peaked by midnight, so I was unconscious or asleep until I was awakened by automatic rifle fire about 5 A.M. The sailors and Coast Guardsmen were back shortly after dawn; Ferdinand stayed behind. The sailors told me that there was no guard posted that night, that the Japs were all sleeping in a thatched lean-to. Our men opened up with everything they had when one of the Japs stepped outside to relieve himself. Sayonara! Another 12 souls in Japanese paradise.

Didn't realize till later that I was grateful for the fever that made me miss that part of the operation.

I don't know what our mission accomplished but it was evidently productive — at least productive enough for the Coast Guard to give their men the Bronze Star. I'd like to have had one too.

*   *   *

September was a pretty rough month, but things got worse in October and November. The balance of power seesawed back and forth between the two powers: The Marines and Air Corps had air superiority during the day which kept the enemy ships away part of the time. Japan still had sea superiority and operated rather freely up and down Ironbottom Sound in the darkness. Their bombers still got through and bombed us about every day for months, sometimes twice a day. I forget the exact number of days, but we were bombed by the Japanese every single day for over 100 days in succession. We kept the number of their air strikes on the bulletin board along with the current baseball and/or football scores we picked up on the shortwave radio.

Oddly enough, those of us at the Operating Base didn't feel very threatened by the bombings. We knew that the Japs were trying to tear up Henderson Field nearly a mile away, so our chances of getting a bomb hit were pretty slim. Fortunately for us, there were no stray bombs in our area. We did take to the foxholes if we were away from the beach; if we were on the beach, we hopped into a boat and headed for open water a few thousand yards out. The closest I ever came to getting hit by a Jap air strike was not by a bomb, but by a falling airplane engine!

We could almost set our watches by the punctuality of the bombers; they always showed up at noon. When the Ferdinand in New Guinea first spotted them, the message was relayed to Henderson. "Condition Yellow" — Jap planes on their way. Half an hour later, "Condition Red" — Jap bombers in sight. That's when we hit the boats or the foxholes. As the bombers approached the field, the Marine fighters were waiting up above and waded into the usual two formations of about 30 planes. It was quite a show watching the fighters attack, then pull back as the bombers neared the target so that the anti-aircraft guns could do their work. We watched and saw the planes in the formation get hit one by one, trailing smoke, losing altitude, and finally crashing into the sea. It wasn't unusual to see half — or more — of the enemy formation shot down before it was over the target only to be further decimated by the accuracy of the anti-aircraft and more were downed by the fighters as they struggled to reach the safety of their base at Rabual in New Britain. On this one particular day, a Jap bomber blew up when an anti-aircraft shell made a direct hit. Its pieces fell into the sea; an engine hit the water close enough to our boat to give us a good shower. The geyser it made shot up into the air 50 feet.

*   *   *

We didn't keep tabs on the number of shellings, but an educated guess would be well in excess of 50. Many nights, the ships — destroyers, cruisers, and even a battleship — would begin shelling while Washing Machine Charlie was cruising overhead. Sometimes he dropped flares to help the ship pinpoint its target. Again, the target was always the airfield. Shellings from sea were pretty much the same; the Japs would come in close, just out of range of our coast artillery. They would shell for 15 minutes to a half hour, then take off. One night was different; boy, was it different! That was the night we got shelled by a Jap battlewagon. She came in close, closer than usual, and opened up with a broadside of 18″ shells. The biggest shell our battlewagons fired was 16″.

I'll never forget the pounding we took. It was late at night so most of us were inside the mosquito nets shootin' the breeze about something (girls, probably) when the Japs fired the first salvo. The sound was deafening and the flash lit up the area like it was noontime. We headed for the foxholes but did not make it before she let go with the second salvo. Again, the noise and the light, but she was firing at such short range that the shells were coming in low, so low that we could feel the heat of them on our bare backs as they sped toward the target. She gave us living hell for nearly 15 minutes and then she was up and gone. We heard later that it took the engineers eight hours to patch up the runway enough to be operable. Everyone at the field, pilots, crews, maintenance, and engineers, worked all night. There were other times when the word went out that Henderson Field had been destroyed, only to have planes landing and taking off there less than three hours later.

*   *   *

Some dumb things also happen in combat, and for a few of us, thanks be to God, they were not fatal. About the dumbest thing I ever pulled, and it was in good faith, happened one day when we were asked to take a company of Raiders (a commando-like group of highly trained and skilled Marines) on what we thought was a routine landing eight or ten miles down the beach behind the Japanese lines. We had maybe a dozen landing craft for the mission. Once we manned the boats, we went to the beach where the Raiders were waiting. Once loaded, I put the boat in reverse and . . . nothing happened; my reverse gear was gone! Knowing that if I told the beachmaster, he would scratch me for that run, I yelled to the boat on my starboard side and threw him a line to pull me into deep water. Fine. We formed a line and headed for the landing area.

There were *not* supposed to be any enemy troops there; the Raiders were there on a reconnaissance mission. But there *were* enemy troops there and just before the boats touched the beach, the shooting started. Lordy mercy, the Japs were shooting at the boats and the Raiders in the boats were shooting back at the Japs, even as they were storming ashore. The gunfire from both sides was deafening and we could see tracer bullets zipping all over the place — and I was in a boat without a reverse gear! The guy who pulled me off the beach when we shoved off had already gone — I was the lone boat on the beach! Fortunately, someone saw me stranded and came back and pulled me free.

Doesn't the Bible say something about the good Lord taking care of little children? Seems like us fearless warriors got a little help there too!

We didn't have a single casualty on the boats, but every craft went back to base with a good number of bullet holes.

*   *   *

On another rescue operation, we were called on to go back to that same area to pick up some Marines who were in what I suppose could be called a "running gun fight" with a Japanese patrol which would not break it off even when the Marines turned and headed for home. If it kept up the way it was going, the Marines would be shooting at the Japs on their tail all the way back to our lines, a good five miles away. Rather than do that, they radioed for rescue boats.

We were told to go to one of our destroyers lying off the beach about a mile offshore. When we got there, the ship's captain sent half the boats in and kept the rest of us in reserve. When the first boat returned to the ship, the Marines were ordered aboard the destroyer. One of the first men to make the climb from the lighter to the ship slipped and fell into the ocean, loaded down with full field gear: pack, rifle, sidearm, grenades, ammo belt — stuff that would weigh at least 70 pounds.

When he hit the water, he went down fast, and I was over the side after him about five seconds later. About six feet down, I saw him and reached out and grabbed a handful of his field pack, *but I could not move him;* all I could do was hang on and work like hell to keep him from going deeper. At the point I thought my lungs would explode, two more bodies knifed down through the water. A couple of sailors from the destroyer saw that we were in trouble, and they stripped and came in for us. When they had a good grip on him, I let go and shot to the surface. We were both pulled aboard the ship in not too bad a shape for the experience we had been through. We both vomited up a gallon (at least) of sea water, then went back to doing what we had been doing before.

I felt sorry for the Marine because he knew how close he had come; it showed on his face even after we were safely aboard the ship. Was it his nearness to death? Or was it because he lost his rifle? I was never in any real danger. I didn't lose anything; all I had to do was let go and come up for air. I wonder what I would have done if the two sailors who came to the rescue had been a few seconds longer? As we were pulling away from the ship on our way back to the base, the Marine made a faint gesture with his hand.

"Thanks."

"No sweat."

Humor —
In and Out of Uniform

A couple of humorous things happened along about this time. The first has to do with the cargo ships that were now coming in regularly, which meant work around the clock until they were empty. Many times, we worked all night if the moonlight was bright enough to operate by without using our running lights.

On this particular occasion, we had been unloading three ships. When the two largest were empty, they weighed anchor and took off. There wasn't too much left on the remaining ship, so our CO gave half of us the rest of the day off. After the hours of sweat and grime, we took a swim in the nude before going back to base to sack out. While we were in the water, someone yelled "TORPEDO!" A Jap submarine had fired a torpedo at the almost-empty ship, but the depth of the torpedo was set at too low a depth, thus it went *under* the ship, continued on in the water toward us and traveled right up on the beach. I wasn't in a position to see it, but one of the guys who was standing knee-deep in the water did—and when he did, he turned and began to run. He ran up the beach out of the water in a straight line inland *with the torpedo right behind,* as if it were chasing him! And momentum brought the torpedo out of the water a good ten feet up onto the beach, high and dry, where it lay in the sand, propeller twirling until it ran out of fuel.

It was quite a sight, watching a Jap torpedo chase a naked young American sailor—and it almost caught him; not more than six feet separated the two when the torpedo lost momentum on the sand. Scuttlebutt had it that American torpedoes exploded after a certain distance traveled (or number of revolutions turned); the Jap torpedoes, however, simply stopped when they ran out of fuel.

In the next weekly newsletter, we got the usual news and ball game scores and standings, but that issue carried a lead story that was headlined: NAKED SAILOR OUTRUNS ENEMY TORPEDO!

Evidently, a war correspondent was on hand to see this because a news blurb about it was quick to hit the national wire services. A couple of people mailed me the clipping from the Lubbock paper.

*   *   *

The other thing had to do with security. Jap patrols penetrated the Marine positions on a number of occasions, reconnaissance missions mostly, so a system of passwords was mandatory. We were told to use words with the letter "L" because the Japanese had great difficulty pronouncing that one particular letter.

The true story goes that one Marine outfit picked the password "Lalla Puluzzie" for that night. (Passwords were changed every night.) The guard on duty was concealed in the brush by the side of a dirt trail when he heard a motor vehicle coming toward him, driving slowly and quietly. As it came closer, the guard yelled out, "Halt. Give the password." The vehicle halted but no password was forthcoming. As instructed, the Marine guard counted to three, then squeezed off a round in the direction of the vehicle.

The Marine driver had momentarily forgotten the password, but when the guard's bullet smashed through his windshield, he hit the ground yelling, "Hallelujah."

Another shot through the glass.

"HALLELUJAH, GODDAMMIT HALLELUJAH."

*   *   *

In November, we got our first ration of beer. It was a great event for the boozehounds in our outfit and their beer-drinking friends, but it didn't mean much to those of us who were younger. Everyone on the island was entitled to two bottles per day as long as it lasted. The master-at-arms issued our beer chits at muster that night; next morning we formed a beer line about a quarter of a mile long. I drank half a bottle of the warm beer, then sold it and the other unopened bottle for $5. A lot of the nondrinkers sold their chits for $5 each.

Here again, the boozehounds came up with what I thought was an ingenious way to have cold beer without refrigeration: They took the beer they wanted to cool and buried it just beneath the surface of the sand. They then went to the Jap fuel dump (where I had been before) and rolled aviation gasoline drums to where the beer was buried and then soaked the sand with gasoline. An hour or so later, the beer they pulled out of the sand was very cold; the bottles frosted up in the humidity. It was cold because of the first principle of refrigeration: Evaporation. Whatever, they kept their secret and made a bundle of money by charging the Marines four bits per bottle for cooling their warm beer.

"Pending Court Martial Proceedings"

My arrest came as a surprise, but not nearly the surprise as the thought of my getting a General Court Martial — then the surprise turning to shock and disbelief when I read the Articles of War concerning my offense and found that it was punishable by "death before a firing squad." I knew what I was doing was wrong, but not that wrong! My only defense was the time-worn excuse, "But everyone else is doing it too."

A succession of events brought it all about.

* * *

In early November of 1942, Japanese ground forces outnumbered the American ground forces for the first time. Consequently, an additional 6,000 American troops were rushed to the island; they arrived on the nights of the 11th and 12th and were landed successfully in spite of heavy enemy air attacks. Once empty, the transports took off immediately, but the escorting force of warships — cruisers and destroyers — stayed behind to cover the beachhead after they learned from a coastwatcher that a big Jap bomber force was on its way to the island. The resulting engagement was called the "First Battle of Guadalcanal." It was another American naval disaster. In it, two American admirals were killed, two cruisers and six destroyers were sunk, and the remaining vessels — all of them — were damaged. The Japs lost two destroyers and a battleship.

"The Second Battle of Guadalcanal" took place a couple of days later, very near the location of the first battle — but this time, the results were reversed: A convoy of 11 Japanese ships carrying 11,000 troops steamed down the Slot — Ironbottom Sound. Prior to the arrival of the transports, nine Japanese destroyers, four cruisers, and two battleships pounded Henderson Field, but not before incoming Marine and Navy fighter-bombers made mincemeat of the Japanese fleet. American losses were sizable, but nothing near that of the Japanese: At dawn, the Jap battlewagon was a blazing inferno (which later sank) and seven of the 11 troop transports had been sunk; the remaining four transports were beached and burning. Only 4,000 of the Jap soldiers made it ashore.

After each of these two major engagements, the sailors of the Operating Base manned their boats and went out to pick up survivors — American survivors. It was a sea of devastation, the entire area covered with a thick layer of oil; all kinds of debris was floating in it with survivors hanging on to whatever they could grab. They were all so black with oil that we had to come in close to see if they were ours or theirs. American survivors took precedence, of course; later in the day we went back out for the Japs but found very few. My boat didn't see any.

We also picked up the dead sailors and the body parts which had been blown away. There were not very many parts, arms and legs, that is. I don't know why, but when arms and legs are blown off, they usually sink — but not the torso; it will float. Doc told us that the torso has cavities which retain and even produce gasses — like the lungs, stomach, bowels, etc. Makes sense.

After a couple of trips (about 15 miles each way), the insides of our boats were as black with oil as the outside. It took weeks of washing them down with gasoline, over and over again, to dissolve it. With a lot of sweat, we got the boats clean. That is, we got the oil and grime off. Funny thing about the blood stains; much of it remained until we repainted the boat.

                    *   *   *

There was one pathetic sight that still haunts me: One of our cruisers was so badly disabled that the captain had sounded the "Abandon Ship," so there was not supposed to be anyone aboard. In addition to the damage done to it by enemy shells, she had also taken a torpedo amidships and deep down, I imagine, because the explosion had evidently broken her keel since bow and stern moved in opposite directions with the current. There was still one person aboard, on the bridge; he was an officer or a chief because he wore khakis (enlisted men wore blue dungarees). We heard the spaced "pop" — "pop" — "pop" from a distance but didn't realize it was rifle fire until we got closer, almost alongside. And when we did, there he was, resting his rifle on the rail of the bridge and shooting the Jap sailors in the water. We yelled at him, trying to get him to come aboard, but he ignored us. We yelled at him to please cease firing, that he may be firing at his own men. When he kept right on, we pulled away from the ship and got between him and the Japs in the water. Fortunately for us, he didn't fire with us in the way. After a while, the crippled cruiser drifted out of range so we headed back to base with our load of oil-covered and bleeding survivors. Never heard anything about what we saw — and don't know what happened to the guy on the bridge doing the shooting.

*   *   *

A week or so before the first battle, we were again on short rations and most of the Navy and Coast Guard personnel were sick and emaciated. Everyone attached to the Operating Base had come down with malaria at least three times and with dengue at least twice. Jungle rot was now a part of what we lived with every day. Each of us had been under heavy pressure working long hours getting critical supplies unloaded when they came in. The ships' skippers yelled at us to hurry it up and the beachmaster yelled at us to hurry it up — and we did the best we could under the circumstances. In addition to the fevers and rot, we were all suffering from diarrhea and or dysentery, so we had adopted an unwritten rule that nobody (and that included the four-man Marine work party) would mess his drawers if it could be prevented; we either took him ashore if he could wait that long or we would stop the boat so that he could drop his drawers and hang his fanny over the side. (That must have presented quite a picture.)

Another unwritten rule was that if we were unloading canned goods (food), we would eat. When the ships came in, we knew pretty well what was in each hold: Food would be unloaded from one hold, machine parts from another, clothing from another, etc. As such, the boats would take turns going to the hold to get a load of food to take ashore. Once the cases and crates of food were aboard, the Marines would go through them to see what goodies we could partake of before we unloaded on the beach. If, for instance, we found a case of peaches, we would break it open and help ourselves and then stow the unopened cans under the sternsheets for future use. A typical run to a ship was like this: We would go to the ship but would have to lay off to the side until the boat or boats ahead of us were loaded. This idle time was chow time if we had any food aboard. Take the peaches, for instance. The Marines would open a gallon can with a bayonet (a clean one, we hoped) and everyone would help himself with the spoon he brought aboard. (Everybody working the incoming ships carried a spoon in his pocket.) This was a common practice, sort of a "privilege" when we worked the food cargo on a ship. "Perks," I suppose you could say.

*   *   *

Back to my arrest and pending court martial...

The reason I used peaches in the afore illustration is that peaches happened to be what we were eating one day as our little boat was bobbing up and down in the water, waiting our turn to go alongside the freighter. Once loaded, we headed back to the beach. I don't remember what our cargo was, but it was not food. When the boat slid up on the beach to get its cargo offloaded, the beach-master, Mr. Deveraux, was there — along with four Marine Military Police. When our cargo was on the truck, he said to the MPs, "Search the boat."

They went immediately to the stern-sheets, the only place on the boat where anything could be stored out of sight, and began to take out its contents: Gallon cans of fruit juices, peaches, pears, apple butter, etc. All told, we probably had 20 gallons stowed away back there.

Since our unit operated independently, this was my first contact with Mr. Deveraux. He was angry but kept his cool when he saw all that foodstuff. He said to the MPs, "Place these men under arrest and put them in the brig. The charge is 'looting.' Charges will be filed for their General Courts Martial."

He then gave us a good tongue-lashing and said that we were to be made "examples of," that this practice was going to stop, and on and on and on. The MP sergeant interrupted and told Mr. Deveraux that there was no brig, only a compound for Japanese prisoners. Mr. Deveraux then took each name, rank, serial number, and outfit; he informed us that we were under "house arrest" and that we were not to leave the immediate area of our tents, mess hall, or latrine without his prior approval.

As other boats came in, they too were searched — without finding a single can of anything. We learned later that a coxswain on another boat which was laying to (and probably eating) had noticed a commotion on the beach, so put his field glasses on the activity and had seen the MPs pull all of our canned goods out. He understandably dumped what he had over the side and got word to the other boats. In any case, ours was the only boat searched that had "contraband" aboard — which made us look bad, indeed. Next day, we heard all kinds of stories about Marines and sailors finding lots of cans of fruits and juices all up and down the beach. (Strangely, some of the cans floated while others sank; it depended on the contents, I suppose.)

That night after chow, everybody came around and wanted to know what happened, etc., and talked about the court martial — which was the part that really worried me. I had made Gunner's Mate, Third Class, not long before, so I didn't want to get busted and I sure as hell didn't want that on my service record. One of the guys — there's one in every outfit — was a "sea lawyer" and knew all about this kind of thing. He told us what would probably happen, but it was so absurd we didn't pay any attention to him. Don't know where he got it, but the next day he had a copy of the Articles of War! There it was, in print, the punishment for looting while in combat, the maximum punishment: "Death by firing squad."

To what degree was Mr. Deveraux going to "make an example" of us? I didn't get much sleep that night — and my CO was no help.

"I'm sorry, but it is out of my hands. I'll do what I can...."

*   *   *

The three of us who were involved in this "looting" thing never saw the work-party Marines again nor heard what happened to them. But for us, it was "business as usual" for a few days; one of us would report to Mr. Deveraux each morning for permission to man the boats. Permission was granted, but we were ordered to stay away from the cargo holds which were unloading food. (What he didn't know was that the food would have been much safer in our boat than in any other!)

After chow one evening a couple of days later, several of us were sitting in and around a tent that had been pitched for recreation (such as card games, writing letters, etc.) when we heard a noise in the distant hillside that sounded something like, "Carrrump!" and was followed by the scream of an artillery shell *coming toward us!* We hit the ground running but not in time to make the foxholes. The shell overshot us by a hundred yards. A few minutes later, another Carrrump — and this one hit in the middle of our tent area. All told that night, "Pistol Pete," as he became known, fired a half-dozen shells at us, probably about 75-millimeter in size. He fired only a few, and quickly, so that he could get his field piece back under cover before his location could be spotted by the Marines, who could have then sent in a team to knock it out. The next night the same thing happened; nothing prolonged; 15 or 20 minutes of firing and no more than a half-dozen rounds, but one of our machine shops was damaged.

The following morning the officers of the base had a staff meeting at which they discussed our latest dilemma. Marine Brass at headquarters said that the Japs had a lone piece of artillery hidden in those hills, probably in a cave, and that they were using it to tear down our morale and to destroy whatever property they could at the same time—and the property we had acquired over the months was considerable. We had machine shops, armory, a small dry dock, and much more that we couldn't afford to have blown up. As such, the decision had been made to move the Naval Operating Base from Kukum Beach to Lunga Point to a spot that was out of range from Pistol Pete. However, they said, a complete move could take as long as a month, moving a little bit over there each day and *still* manning the boats and doing business as usual.

Problem was, infiltrating Japs might possibly sabotage what was left behind if Pistol Pete didn't get it first, and if it wasn't sabotaged it would probably be carried away by the Marines. (Pilfering Marines, and in combat, mind you!) The present site would have to be guarded, of course. The three Navy pilferers, having discussed this possibility beforehand, immediately stepped forward to bravely accept the challenge even before volunteers were asked for. It made us look good, but bravery in the face of enemy shelling had nothing to do with it. We were afraid of Mr. Deveraux. We figured that if we could keep out of his sight for a while and if we did a passable job of "minding the store" that our CO might put in a good word that would get the court martial dropped. He could say something about what we did in staying was "beyond the call of duty" or some other such high-sounding phrase, just anything that would get us off the hook.

*   *   *

The whole outfit—minus us three—packed personal gear and loaded it on the truck for Lunga Point and moved out within the hour. A truck or two came back each day to collect what was needed for priority work. At the rate they were going, it would take three weeks to get it all moved. Meanwhile, we three stayed in camp with nothing to do but keep our eyes open, although we did go out and

The beach at Lunga Point. While Marines unload artillery canisters and runway baffle from the boat in the foreground, others board in the background for another sortie behind the Japanese lines. *Photo credit:* **Ralph Morse,** *Life Magazine* ©. **Time Warner Inc.**

work the boats occasionally. It was okay to leave the area during the day as long as one guy was left behind on guard duty. We did prevent the foodstuffs from going to the Marines, and other materiel too, I'm sure. Fortunately, we had plenty to read and we played lots of gin rummy. But with Pistol Pete, his routine never varied: Late every afternoon, just before dusk, out would come his cannon for the half-dozen rounds he would lob at us. He always missed us— except once.

*   *   *

It was about a week after the "siege" started that we had run out
of clean clothing, so late one afternoon, we stopped one of the
native scouts who was looking for a Raider outfit and paid him a
pack of cigarettes and two chocolate bars to take two jerry-cans to
the Tenaru River and fill them with fresh water. While we were
standing there in our skivvies waiting for the water, we heard the
scream of an incoming shell, then the familiar WHAM! Here's Old
Pete again, but this time he's too damn close, this shell not more
than 50 yards away. We were in our foxholes before it hit. I didn't
know why, but I did not have a positive feeling about the outcome
of the shelling. Sure enough, we heard the next one coming and we
found that you can hear the scream of a shell that is coming directly
at you — because we heard the one that got us. Actually, it hit the
ground about 6 feet from the entrance of our foxhole. The concussion was horrible; it not only knocked us over on our sides (we were
in a sitting position) but blew us toward the rear of the foxhole. We
were covered with sand; it was in our hair, eyes, ears, and mouth.
We came close to being buried alive. The next round we also heard;
it hit the part of the top, but that blast was no worse than the first.
I remember the falling sand and felt a kind of vertigo as we were being tossed around from wall to wall and bouncing against each
other — and I remember thinking at the time how lucky we were to
have covered the top of our hole so well with coconut logs and an
extra layer of sandbags. That little precaution might have saved
lives.

*   *   *

After a while (it seemed like forever) the shelling stopped, so we
crawled out of that hole. It was difficult to see with so much sand
in our eyes and our hearing was impaired by the concussion. The
other guy's nose was smashed and he had red, angry-looking welts
on his nose and left cheek that were later swollen and beautiful hues
of black and blue, but otherwise we were all right — except for our
hearing. Our ears hurt like hell and we were almost deaf, so had to
really speak out to be heard. It took a couple of weeks for our hearing to gradually come back, but it was never as good as it was before.
I don't know about the other guys, but from the moment of that
blast, my ears began ringing, loudly — and to this day the ringing has
never stopped. It was a bother for a few years, but I had to get used
to it. It seems that I have experienced more and more hearing loss

as the years have gone by, but I don't suppose I'll ever be deaf; my "Guadalcanal ringing" will always be with me.

Since we had been so bounced around by the force of the shells and were temporarily deaf, the Exec thought our getting a Purple Heart would be automatic, that we had in fact been wounded and had been treated for that wound by a Navy corpsman. When he was asked to submit the required form, the corpsman wouldn't do it.

"Sorry, sir, but regulations say that to qualify for a PH, you gotta be wounded, and to be wounded means you gotta bleed. No blood, no Purple Heart. Those are the rules I hafta go by."

* * *

The Japanese fighting forces who were not engaged in the "Second Battle of Guadalcanal," specifically its air force, knew that the invasion force of 11,000 men reinforcing the 25,000 seasoned soldiers already entrenched around the American forces would easily take Henderson Field the morning of November 15th — especially after the heavy bombardment from the battlewagons and cruisers the night before. Somewhere along the Japanese line, there was a breakdown in communication, because it was apparent that their air force did not know of the heavy losses suffered during the night because their planes came in for a landing the next morning!

Our decision to stay with the old campsite meant we also had to prepare most of our own meals; the new base on Lunga Point was too far away for us to come and go three times a day and there was not always a vehicle available to run over to us. We had plenty of staples on hand, so had to go over only a time or two for bread, powdered eggs, and anything special the cooks might have on hand. We decided to go early one morning because we didn't get much sleep the night before. We were awakened sometime during the night by constant pounding of gunfire — *big* gunfire — at sea. Somebody was sure pounding hell outa somebody else. We had heard pounding of this kind before and we always figured that we were giving the Japs hell. I don't recall a single time that I thought we might lose the island and be killed or captured, even though the month before we had been instructed where to go and what to do "in case the Japanese overrun the Marine positions."

We were up by dawn, got dressed and were about ready to leave when all hell broke loose again, this time around Henderson Field. Over the gunfire, we heard the sound of a multi-engine aircraft before we saw it, and ten seconds later, there it was, a Japanese medium bomber headed straight for us at a height of no more than a hundred feet — just over the tops of the coconut trees. Apparently, the Jap air corps thought the airfield was now in Japanese control because this plane came in to make a normal landing. When everything around the airstrip opened up on them, they pulled up and were trying to gain altitude to get away over the ocean.

We saw her over the trees just in time for me to step inside the tent for my Browning automatic rifle, which I kept loaded for just such an occasion as this (although I never expected it to occur); all I had to do was snap the safety off and pick up a bandoleer of extra clips. Not knowing what I might be shooting at when I loaded them, I had a combination of tracers, armor-piercing, and copper-jacketed shells. That way, I could see where my shots were going and knew that some of them would pierce lightweight armor. I took three steps to a tree and leveled my rifle against it and sighted in on the plane, then squeezed the trigger — and kept it squeezed. In about three seconds, all 20 of the shells ripped through the fuselage in the area of the cockpit. She continued to fly for perhaps a thousand yards, then sort of peeled to the left and crashed in a grove of palm trees. There was an explosion but no fire.

Did *I* shoot it down? I don't know, but I doubt it, because there must have been 50 Marines up and down that beach who were also firing their rifles — and even pistols — into that slow-moving behemoth up there. Someone said it was a Betty-class bomber. I didn't ask to be credited with shooting it down, and after going over to the crash site, I guess that's the reason why. We saw only two bodies. (Rather, parts of bodies. One had been torn in half at the waist; the other was just an unrecognizable mass of mangled flesh and broken bones still strapped to his seat in the cockpit.) Funny how important it was at age 19 that I get in on the action and "get me a Jap," and how, after that dreamed-of action came true, I didn't want any part of the credit for having killed the crew of an enemy plane.

*   *   *

My shooting for the day wasn't over. We had something to eat: Hardtack with some apricot preserves and coffee. It wasn't too bad if you let the hot coffee soften up the hardtack a little before you started to chew. Back at the tent, I thought I should clean my rifle, but thought better of it; there was too much activity on the beach and at the airfield. With all the commotion at sea last night, then the bomber this morning, what the hell's going on?

I had no sooner asked the question when Henderson Field opened up, again — and this time it was firing *on* and being fired *at:* A Jap fighter — a Zero — roared low over the field with both wing-guns blazing, strafing the field. Again we had a Jap plane headed straight in and flying low; he looked like he was trying to fly straight into the tree where I was standing. He peeled off to the left at the exact moment I pulled the trigger on the Browning, emptying the clip. All 20 shells slammed into the fuselage of the plane, up near the cockpit. Hot on his tail came another Zero, in the same pattern. Again all the Marines in the area were firing their rifles and pistols, but this time there was no kill. Both planes circled and came back in for another run, but changed course for a new target, out of our range when they peeled off this time.

* * *

I don't remember how long we "stood guard" in that empty camp, but it was probably between two and three weeks. Other than Pistol Pete at work, it was pretty good duty — except at night. In the beginning, we took turns; one of us would stay awake until about midnight, then awaken another to take over till about 4 A.M., and then the third man stayed up the rest of the night. We started out this way, but with nobody in charge, the system broke down. For one thing, we were awakened, off and on, all night. We were very conscious of being alone and vulnerable — and the coconut crabs didn't help.

A coconut crab is a big bugger, a scavenger that feeds on old coconuts. He's nocturnal, so he comes out only late at night to feed, but before he can feed, he has to tear the husk off the old coconut and then break the shell. The few Marines who made the mistake of catching a crab with bare hands suffered multiple broken bones and deep lacerations. I saw one sailor with multiple compound fractures. You can well imagine being awakened in the middle of the night by these loud, grinding noises that sounded very much like the Japanese army charging through the jungle. Horrible sound. We never got used to it, even when we were back on Tulagi and were relatively secure.

* * *

Part of the Japanese army did march through our camp one night. We didn't know how many, but knew it was at least one soldier. We were awakened next morning by the sound of voices, two Marines talking. We got up and went outside to find out what was going on. The Marines were discussing how they were going to repair the telephone lines that were strung high in the coconut trees that ran alongside our tent area. During the night the Japanese had infiltrated a Marine position and had come into our area to cut the lines; they picked a tree strung heavy with lines not more than 50 feet from where we were sleeping. He (or they) came through our camp, climbed a tree, cut the lines, then climbed back down and disappeared back into the bush. That was too close for comfort. When our CO heard about it, he ordered us to pack our gear and rejoin the outfit. And we were ready!

*   *   *

We were still skittish about the court martial, so asked our CO what we should do about Mr. Deveraux.

"Oh, him." He smiled and said, "He and his outfit got shipped out last week. I wonder if he left anything with the new CO on you guys?"

He had not.

What a blessed relief!

About 20 years later we lived in Honolulu and attended the Church of the Holy Nativity in Aina Haina. We became friends with a couple there and saw them socially a few times. He was a Coast Guard rear admiral, the commandant of that Coast Guard district. At a luau one evening, Admiral Vellis was telling a story about something funny that happened at the office and in the telling mentioned his executive officer, a captain named Deveraux. I asked if this Captain Deveraux was ever on Guadalcanal.

"As a matter of fact, he was. He was the beachmaster on the invasion."

I told the admiral about the looting and court martial and asked him to remember me to Captain Deveraux. He did — and the captain remembered the incident! I intended to go by his office to talk with him, but never did. I still don't know if he did what he did to scare us and the other boat crews or if things just got so hairy that he didn't get around to following through. Whatever. We were much more cautious in our clandestine actions from that point on.

Tulagi – Again

Beginning in late November, the war-weary troops were moving out and the fresh replacements were moving in. General Vandergriff and his 1st Marines were replaced by the 2nd Marines and two Army divisions, commanded by General Patch. In December, we got moved out too, back to Tulagi; we replaced the personnel at the Naval Operating Base there! It was ludicrous; the guys we were replacing had replaced *us* at NOB Tulagi when we were ordered to Guadalcanal. Now we were replacing our replacements so they could go home! Our CO was unhappy, we were unhappy, so all kinds of letters got written to get us some relief—all to no avail. A chief in personnel told our chief that they had to give the combat troop priority . . . that since we were noncombatants we would have to take our turn.

Our turn? When we replace our replacements? This was a beautiful example of what SNAFU really means.

There was one concession: We were all granted R&R time in New Zealand—15 days' worth!

*   *   *

We worked as two sections of 60 men each, so the section chiefs cut the cards to see who would go first. The other section won but it was no big deal; we would go as soon as they came back. About five days before they came back, our CO told us at muster that morning that Admiral Halsey had put out a directive that all overseas R&R had been canceled until further notice. The reason, as it was put to us, had something to do with the assault on Tarawa. Halsey's staff put out the word that all hands would be preparing for the big assault or some such nonsense like that. It didn't make sense to us, but Halsey sitteth on the right hand of Nimitz and could therefore do no wrong. . . . We felt sorry for ourselves, of course, but not more so than the section coming back from New Zealand. We had been through so much rough stuff together that they wanted us to have as much fun and fresh milk as they had enjoyed for two weeks. Once back to duty, they talked very little about their great R&R

because they didn't want to make us feel any worse than we already felt. And when they did talk, it wasn't about girls and sex, it was about sleeping in a real bed without worrying about planes dropping bombs and ships shooting shells, it was about sleeping late and having fresh eggs for breakfast and T-bone steaks for dinner and other sensual stuff like that.

*   *   *

Our return to Tulagi — to the same house we occupied before — was pretty much of a letdown. All the troops there were fresh, and the duty of maintaining a near-peacetime base was very humdrum after our activity of the past few months. We felt a little more civilized, for some reason, with ships in and out of the harbor all the time. We even had electric lights and spent many nights playing cards and listening to Tokyo Rose on our radio. She not only told us how badly we were losing the war, but she also entertained us with the latest stateside music — current songs from the Lucky Strike Hit Parade. And the news she reported was fantastic. After a sea battle, she would tell us the names of OUR ships that were sunk and the full names of their commanding officers! And it was the Americans who had broken the Japanese code.

Time hung heavy because we had been in the combat zone a long time and we were sick, all of us — some to a greater degree than others. I'm not sure, but I think every man in our outfit had malaria and most had had it more than once, and almost all had been down with dengue and diarrhea/dysentery. We all had scars from scratching the jungle rot. We scratched until we bled but that didn't stop us because the more it bled the worse it itched.

*   *   *

There was one unusual twist or left-handed distinction of some kind: We were the only veterans in the Tulagi area who had seen combat, so the new sailors and Marines came to us to hear war stories — and we told them some beauties! The favorite story was so believably told that we almost believed it ourselves! We concocted a yarn about a Japanese troop transport that ran aground on the far end of the island, where the Japanese field headquarters were located. The Marines made a night raid on the headquarters, but first went aboard the grounded ship — which was not a troop transport at all; it was a floating whorehouse. The Japanese did this frequently, we told the wide-eyed newcomers, to keep up the troops' morale. We got so good at telling this tale that it became very believable. Stories about the Imperial Japanese Nookie Fleet became a part of the lore of that campaign!

*   *   *

By early 1943, we heard that there were about 50,000 fresh American troops in the Solomons (plus 120 weary sailors!) while the Japanese were trying to muster an offensive with their 25,000 tired and sick soldiers. We learned after the war that on January 3, 1943, Japanese Imperial Headquarters in Tokyo had conceded defeat at Guadalcanal and given orders for all remaining troops to be evacuated immediately. The "immediately" took a while, since the Americans had air and sea superiority in the area. The Japanese had to evacuate their troops at night; destroyers would sneak in and leave with a couple of hundred or so of the 12,000 sick, weary, and defeated soldiers, then barrel out to sea to be as far away from American fighters and bombers as possible before daylight.

Word was passed on February 7, 1943, that the last enemy soldier had been evacuated from Guadalcanal!

*   *   *

The war was over in the Solomons, but not for us. We stayed in Tulagi, worked the Operating Base, and waited for some action on the many letters that our CO was continually grinding out. At long last, one (or some) of that correspondence got someone's attention. Orders came saying that we were to "proceed on the next available surface transportation to the Receiving Station, U.S. Naval Base, Espireto Santo, New Hebrides."

Back to the New Hebrides

With all the ship traffic in and out of the Solomons, we didn't have to wait long. Tons of supplies were coming in every day, supplies that the rear echelon which was now Guadalcanal would stockpile for future assaults on the chain of islands leading up to the Sea of Japan. It was incredible, the things they brought in—trucks, tanks, bulldozers and tractors, ammunition and powder, cannons and rifles, sophisticated and complete hospital supplies to stock huge multi-bed field hospitals, food—and I could go on and on.

Our replacements were already on board, so we immediately phased ourselves out of any further activity in the Solomons, then spent some time looking forward to just the right ship to get us out of there. Our "dream ship" picked us up on March 5, 1943; we left the Solomons in pretty much the same way we came in: We boarded an almost-empty cargo carrier that had stateroom space enough to accommodate about 200 passengers, four to a stateroom.

Thus, just over seven months after we arrived, we left the Solomons; ours was the longest hitch of any unit that served there during the combat era. The only tears shed at leaving were tears of joy!

I don't remember the name of the ship we boarded, but she was a doozey. We could sleep as late as we wanted, but had to be in the chow hall by 0830 if we wanted breakfast; we ate fresh eggs sunny side up, and drank fresh milk (it had been frozen or powdered, I could never tell which) and had pie with every meal if we wanted it—even at breafast. No duties were assigned; we read, talked, played cards, napped, or sat quietly, gazing out on the beautiful South Pacific Ocean. We stopped in the Santa Cruz Islands for a few days to leave supplies, so had time ashore to lie on the white beaches and play in the surf. There were movies aboard every night. All told, we were aboard 10 beautiful days. Kinda hated to go ashore in the New Hebrides. Our time aboard, I imagined, was pretty much like being on a cruise ship.

*   *   *

128

New Hebrides had really changed: There were dozens of ships of all kinds tied up in the channel, and temporary buildings dotted the shoreline as far as we could see. Counting the crews aboard ship, there had to be at least 100,000 personnel there.

We reported in to the Receiving Station and were assigned bunk space in a very nice Quonset hut, the first one we had ever seen. Life was easy there, but nothing to compare with the ship. For three of us, though, orders came three days later. "Report to the Commanding Officer, USS *Dixie.*"

The *Dixie?* Yecht! She was anchored there in the channel, and had been for six months. The *Dixie* was a destroyer tender; she wasn't supposed to go to sea except to go from one anchorage to another. She had to be in a safe spot for destroyers to come for supplies and repairs. When we reported aboard, she had six destroyers tied up alongside, four of which had been badly damaged in combat.

When we reported in, there were no assignments for us; we were called "supernumeraries." All we had to do was stay out of everybody's way. The ship's complement numbered about 1,200 men. Whatever the number, there were exactly 47 more men aboard than they had sleeping space for. We three new arrivals joined 44 others who were assigned to sleep in the mess hall! It worked like this: After the second nightly movie we could swing our hammocks and crawl in for the night *after* the deck apes cleaned and swept down after the movie—which was usually near midnight. Not long after going to sleep, we were awakened at 0430 to get our hammocks rolled and stowed so that the mess cooks could break out the tables and get them set up for chow, beginning at 0600.

After two nights of this, I began looking for a spot on deck to lay my weary head, but there was none! Hundreds of sailors, it seemed, were sleeping on every available open space on deck!

Fortunately, I had to endure the *Dixie* for only ten more days. The three of us from the old outfit were called to personnel and given orders to report back to the receiving station to rejoin the old outfit. We were at Receiving Station Espireto Santo six more weeks, then got orders on June 1st to report to the Section Base on Ile Nou, New Caledonia.

New Caledonia

N ew Caledonia is a French colony; the capital city is Noumea, whose prewar population was about 25,000, mostly Frenchmen, plus a fairly large native population. We were told there were natives but I never saw one. The Section Base (which is very much like an operating base) was on Ile Nou, about three miles from the main island. Originally, Ile Nou housed a large prison population of what the French called the "incorrigibles," a junior-sized Devil's Island, I suppose you could say. There were a few prisoners still housed there, but no locks on the cells; the prisoners were free to come and go as they pleased. Shortly after the war began, the worst of the incorrigibles were taken to another prison, probably Guiana. The prisoners left behind had been "pardoned" or some such term which meant they were free to live among the civilian population on the island, but they were not free to leave it or to return to France. They stayed on in the prison, we were told, because they were not accepted by the people in Noumea; they were regarded as and treated like lepers.

The prison was located in the center of Ile Nou; the Section Base with its excellent docking facilities was located on the south end of the island; the Naval Air Station with its newly constructed runways was located on the north end. The prison was very interesting: There was one big, three-storied main building that contained the cells; there were several smaller buildings that had once been used for shops, guards' quarters, etc. — and the entire complex was surrounded by a ten-foot stone wall that had jagged pieces of glass set in concrete on the top. In the courtyard of the prison, in a very prominent spot, stood a guillotine, complete and in good working order! I had never seen one before. The prisoners who still lived there were mostly old men, some in their dotage. They worked in their gardens, hand carved rosaries for the Catholic sailors, and for a few francs, they would give a tour of the prison. They pointed out, very proudly, the dark stains on the platform of the guillotine where the heads fell; blood permeated the wood from dozens of executions. One tour of the prison was enough.

I don't know why we were moved from Tulagi; we were pulling exactly the same duty on Ile Nou, except that our billets were not nearly so comfortable and we had much more responsibility with fewer hands to meet it. Even so, we were not under the kind of pressures that had dogged us in combat. Since I was a gunner's mate, I was assigned to the armory where we had a large collection of weaponry that was never used nor asked for. Nevertheless, we cleaned each piece—from a Smith and Wesson 38-caliber Police Special all the way up to a 20-millimeter cannon. We never had enough to do in the armory, so it became a favorite hangout for anyone who dropped by for coffee—and there was always a card game.

It was a pity that I didn't drink, because we got more booze, and I mean good whiskey, than we could ever consume. Problem was, we couldn't let anyone else on the base—or anywhere else—know we had it because of the way it was obtained. Amazing how the word gets around to merchant sailors, even during a war. A merchant sailor whose ship was unloading in Noumea came to the armory one day looking for small-arms ammunition, 22-caliber and 45-caliber, for target practice while their freighter was under way. We had hundreds of cases of ammo stockpiled but not one single case had ever been requested, legally or illegally, until now. The chief made a deal: A case of ammo for a case of whiskey. We traded, quietly and confidentially, but the merchant sailor, of course, told a sailor on another ship who told another sailor on another ship . . . and soon we had a bootlegging enterprise going that would have made a big-time Prohibition Era operator jealous.

If the other guys on base found out we had whiskey, we'd be in trouble, so we kept it to ourselves and drank a little of it and sold a little, and the whiskey kept coming in. Those merchant sailors kept bringing it and we kept trading until we had so many cases of good whiskey we didn't have places to hide it. In desperation, we altered the trade a little bit: We continued to trade, case for case, but we kept the empty ammo cases. We could get most of a case of whiskey in an empty ammo case which we would then hide in the ammunition dump along with the full cases of live ammunition!

Where did the merchant sailors get all that good whiskey? The cargo manifest on a merchantman was common knowledge, so an enterprising sailor could rework the cargo hold while the ship was under way. Putting a few cases in an out-of-the-way place was not difficult. A shortage in the manifest? Breakage, or it was stolen from the pier before all the cargo was loaded.

Don't know how the situation was resolved because I got shipped out about the time the problem became acute. We had a small fortune in liquid assets stored in that ammunition dump.

* * *

We hadn't been at the Section Base very long when I began to think more and more about what the sailor in personnel at Henderson Field said. "Go to the first Naval Air Station you come to *outside* the combat zone. . ."

I was ready to go by 0800 the next morning — shaved, showered, fresh-pressed dungarees, and clean combat boots. Navy flight school, HERE I COME! I couldn't eat breakfast, but that happens sometimes when I'm excited about something. I left about 0900, walking the three quarters of a mile to the Naval Air Station on the far side of the prison. Halfway there, at the prison, I had to sit down in the shade and rest. When I reported in and told the yeoman what I was there for, he told me that I'd have to wait and talk to the Personnel Officer, that he was in a meeting.

"Sit over there and read a magazine. Coffee's in the next room."

I haven't the faintest idea how long I sat there, but I knew what was coming on. If the personnel officer would just come in, our business wouldn't take more than ten minutes, and I could get somewhere and lie down. I waited a few more minutes and realizing how bad off I was, I told the yeoman that I'd be back in a couple of days — and that's all I remember. I awakened the next day in a bed on the USS *Solace,* a hospital ship.

The medic on duty read me my record and told me that I had passed out at the Air Station, that my temperature had been extremely high. I had been taken to the station sick bay, but the doctor on duty didn't know what I had, so transferred me to the hospital ship because I was "so emaciated." Well, not bad. A couple of days rest sure won't do me any harm.

That afternoon, they gave me a general physical; when I stepped on the scale, it topped out at 118 pounds. The doctor made light of it, said that I wasn't underweight, that my 6′ 4″ was too tall for the weight I carried. And then he ordered a lot of blood work, X-rays, and all that stuff. That night when I went to chow, again I couldn't eat, so I went back to my bunk and lay there until the doctor made evening rounds. He looked at me and had a nurse put a thermometer in my mouth. I was freezing to death. A lab technician came in for blood before I passed out — and I slept until I heard some commotion early the next morning. When the doctor made his rounds, he told me that the lab had been unable to identify the strain of malaria I had, so there would be no medication until they could identify it, and that the strain could be detected only in the blood during an attack.

Thanks, doc, I needed that!

That fever burned on me every single night, beginning at about 1800 hours, for three consecutive nights — four attacks in all. The only thing I got for it was a sympathetic word. For some reason, they weren't giving me anything to stop it until they could identify the strain of the virus. Big deal. I don't know whether they found the strain or not, but they finally started giving me Atabrine along with the IVs I had been getting (I couldn't even force food down).

* * *

A day or so after my admission to the hospital ship, a small white ship came alongside to offload the wounded from a battle that had taken place somewhere up the Solomon chain. I was in no shape to go topside to watch what was going on but the guys who were ambulatory did — and they came back a little green around the gills from just seeing the condition the wounded were in. The USS *Solace* got the bad cases; the less serious went to shore station hospitals to be flown back to the States on the next available planes. The ones we got were all too seriously wounded to travel until their conditions stabilized. Too, almost all had received only rudimentary treatment in field hospitals, so the rest of the patching up had to be done on the hospital ship.

Two of the incoming wounded were placed in the empty bunks in our bay. One of them was in real bad shape; both legs had been blown off, one at the knee and the other at mid-calf, and his legs and buttocks had been pretty well shredded by shrapnel. The other guy had two small bandages on his face, one on either side of his mouth. From outward appearances, his face was swollen but he didn't appear to be seriously wounded for a man who had taken a sniper's 25-caliber bullet through the face.

Poor guy. He couldn't talk and he couldn't eat anything except liquid and pureed foods — and only then with great difficulty. He was in a good amount of pain when they got him settled in the bunk next to mine, so he was given a sedative of some kind. Morphine, probably. Whatever it was, it not only eased the pain but also put him on a narcotic high that made him love the world and want to talk, but since he couldn't talk, he wrote. He wrote crazy things on that little Red Cross pad of paper, much of which was almost illegible or incomprehensible. Crazy things. He rambled on about everything until we started asking him specific questions.

"What happened to you?"

"Was on point. Got shot by a Jap sniper."

"What happened?"

"Got shot, dammit, got shot in the face."

That's all he wanted to say on the subject, so he put his Red Cross tablet down and let the morphine take over.

The hospital corpsman on that afternoon shift was a first class petty officer named Doc, a superb human being. He was about 30, tall, and what hair he had left was a ruddy red as was his full-lip, bushy mustache. Not only was he a competent corpsman, but he was also a man who cared. He didn't say a lot, but his attitude and manner made you feel that you were the only patient on the entire ship that he was concerned with or cared about.

After the Marine was asleep, we made a beeline to Doc to find out what had happened and how badly he was hurt.

Doc told us that he was point man on a patrol when it happened. He was on his stomach at the top of a rise, scanning the terrain ahead when he heard the shot. At that same instant, something stung him on the face and his mouth filled with something that tasted salty. He turned and spat, and when he did, out came blood, broken teeth, and small particles of flesh. The sniper was apparently on the ground adjacent to him on the left when he fired. The lone bullet entered the lower right part of his cheek at exactly the place where you would normally expect to find a dimple. The bullet knocked out two lower teeth, creased the top of his tongue, shot out another lower tooth, then exited at the exact opposite spot on his right cheek! He was brought to the *Solace* not because of the seriousness of his wound, but because there was an oral surgeon aboard who could take out the roots of the broken teeth, suture the deep trough across the middle of his tongue, and stitch the two small holes on either side of his face. He was in surgery a little over an hour.

When the swelling went down, he looked like everybody else except for those two small scabs on his dimples. He asked, by way of his yellow tablet, to be put in for two Purple Hearts — one for each hole.

The other Marine put in our bay was a far different story; that kid was in real bad shape. After Doc had him settled in the bunk, he gave him a pretty hefty shot of morphine, enough to make him sleep for a couple of hours. He was disoriented when he awakened.

"Where in hell am I?"

"On a hospital ship, Mac. You okay?"

"Yeah, but I hurt a little."

"I'll go get Doc."

He wouldn't let me, but he wanted me to stay close to his bunk. It was easy to see that he was scared, not of anything in particular, but just scared. I pulled up a chair and sat there by him for a long time, neither of us talking. I looked at him while he stared at the ceiling. Finally, it became apparent that he wanted to talk but didn't know how to begin. So I did.

"What happened? Step on a land mine?"

"No. Grenade. One of ours."

"OURS? What the hell happened?"

"We were on patrol when we were damn near ambushed by some Japs. We took cover and dug in. When the Japs started moving, one of the replacement boots behind me threw a grenade. Threw it too high. Hit a tree limb and fell in my hole. At my feet, I guess."

He talked for the better part of an hour without my interrupting him even once. I've never heard anything like it, before or since. He was reliving that patrol with me and in so doing, I was carried along with him; I felt that I had been with him all along, even when the grenade tore his legs off. Doc saw what was happening, saw that the pain was back. After he went back to the nursing station, I could see the tenseness fade away as the new shot of morphine did its work. I had nightmares with my fever that night. Whole companies of boot replacements were throwing hand grenades, and they were all falling in my foxhole.

The kid was in better spirits the next morning but still scared half to death. He was scheduled for early surgery; the orthopedic surgeons were going to reopen the wounds on the stumps, take off bone ends, if necessary, then close the wounds in such a way that there would be "pads" of flesh over the bone, a buffer for the prosthesis he would wear for the rest of his life. Doc told us that the shrapnel had left deep lacerations on the inside of his thighs and especially his buttocks, but it appeared that those wounds had been satisfactorily cleaned and sutured at the aid station.

Being scheduled for morning surgery on a hospital ship with dozens of combat wounded was not very definitive. You were lucky if they got to you as scheduled — or even on the same day, much less morning or afternoon. Worst always comes first.

The kid was nervous. We did our best to cheer him up, but we were probably making things worse. Doc, bless his heart, saw and heard what was going on. Making his rounds with medication, he stopped at the kid's bed.

"Did they tell you about the Sea Marine they brought in here that had been blown off a cruiser when it took two torpedo hits?"

He shook his head.

"When we got him, he was one shot-up Marine, still unconscious when he went to surgery and out for 12 hours after they finished patching him up. Pretty sick guy, so they put him in a private room.

"The guy wakes up, finally, and all he can see is white, the white overhead. He tries to move but he can't; both legs are in a cast. He tries to pull himself up but can't; one arm is in a cast. Finally, with his good arm, he finds the call button and presses it."

In comes the nurse. "Welcome back to the world," she says.

"Where in the hell am I?" the Marine tries to say through clenched teeth; he can't get his mouth open to say it.

"Well," the nurse says, "you've been banged up pretty bad, but the medics have taken good care of you. Both legs are broken and in a cast and one arm is broken. You'll heal, but it will take time."

"What's wrong with my mouth? Why can't I open it?"

"Your jaw has been broken; your teeth have been wired together."

"How I am going to eat?"

"Well," the nurse said, "there are three ways we can feed you. We can remove your front teeth and feed you soft food, or we can feed you intravenously, or we can feed you with a tube, rectally. What do you prefer?"

"I sure don't want to lose these teeth and I hate needles. Feed me rectally."

"Very well. Is there anything I can do for you?"

"Yeah," he grunted through clenched teeth. "I want a cup of coffee."

The nurse left the room and returned with a tray holding a cup of coffee, a cream pitcher, and a sugar bowl — and a hose attached to a bag.

"Cream and sugar?" she asked.

"Just a little sugar."

The nurse poured the coffee into the bag, added a spoonful of sugar, and held it up as she inserted the hose into the Marine's anus. No sooner had the liquid began to flow, the Marine began to scream through his clenched teeth.

"Oh, OH, no more, no more."

The nurse immediately yanked the tube out.

"Was it too hot?"

"No," the Marine rasped, "too sweet."

The kid laughed, real big, for the first time. While the smile was still on his face, two medics pushing a gurney came through the door. The kid waved to us as they took him out of the bay.

I guess they put him in another ward when they finished. We never saw nor heard from him again.

*   *   *

A few days later, the doctor came in and told me that there was a ship in the harbor taking the walking wounded back to the States and that I would be going over to it at noon. It was a Dutch ship, the motor ship *Boschfontaine,* a freighter equipped to carry a couple of hundred passengers. I remember sitting on that ship for a couple of days before she sailed while she took on a load of nickel ore at a pier in Noumea.

Don't know why I can't remember much about the three-week trip home, but I only have bits and pieces. I suppose it's because I had another attack of fever while on board. At the end of the long journey home, I still weighed in at 118 pounds.

Well, so much for the Naval Aviation Cadet program!!

San Francisco

T he ship docked at Mare Island, the big Navy Yard just outside San Francisco. At the hospital there, we were given intense physical exams. I hope the blood they took from all of us went to the blood bank. Those of us who came back on the *Boschfontaine* got lots of attention from lots of doctors. One physician I saw often was the specialist in tropical diseases. After a week of tests, I was told that I had a 30-day sick leave coming up soon and would have orders to report back to the hospital at the Naval Air Station, Corpus Christi.

*   *   *

Before there was any leave, or any liberty, we were quarantined for seven days. I don't know why we were quarantined unless the medics thought we might have had something communicable. Or perhaps the hospital needed that much time to test, diagnose, and treat what we had brought back with us. Whatever, we were a motley-looking crew. We wondered how corpsmen, guys we had never seen before, could tell immediately that we were just back from the Southwest Pacific. It was an easy recognition because we all had one thing in common: dermatology problems. One of the corpsmen referred to the survivors of the jungle warfare as a "dermatologist's dream" because most of what we had was "rare," "unusual," or a "new strain" of something. What we brought back were not case studies out of a medical journal. Just about every sailor and Marine who returned from the bush had visible signs of a jungle rot of some kind; some of it was now only scar tissue while some was still active. Scratching a lot was a dead giveaway. Even the scar tissue itched.

*   *   *

During that week of confinement, we spent a considerable amount of time at the ship's store getting re-outfitted; new everything, the sea bag and hammock and all that stuff that went with it. Shoes were still a problem but I knew I could find a pretty close fit on my first liberty—and I had the money. I had been paid only twice in the last year, so I had several hundred dollars of back pay on the books.

Stateside Liberty

T he first liberty back in the States was memorable. I wanted to go to San Francisco alone that first time because I knew what a hassle it was going to be, trying to find a pair of shoes that fit and also passed inspection. None of the guys I knew from the hospital ship would get very excited about spending the afternoon shopping for another guy's shoes, so I left alone, in the early afternoon, wearing my Navy-issue pair of 12B clodhoppers. Like Chicago, it took all afternoon, but it was worth it. And only ten bucks too. The clerk was a female, the first female shoe salesman I had ever had. She wrote out the sales slip. The cashier took my money and asked for something I had never heard of.

"What in the world is a Shoe Stamp?"

She and the salesman were both a little embarrassed, but they filled me in on this wartime regulation that was foreign to me.

"You mean to tell me that I've got to go before the Ration Board and apply for a permit to buy this pair of shoes that the United States Navy is unable to provide?"

It wasn't very long until everybody in the store, salesmen and customers, were aware of my problem — and each had his own opinion; all were sympathetic and vocal.

"What a shame that our fighting men come back home and have to be treated like this, especially when they've been in combat and all..."

Just about the time I was ready to take off my new shoes and go in pursuit of the Ration Board, the casher shrieked.

"Hey, lookie here. I found this old shoe stamp stuck back here in the cash register where we keep the hot checks. It's still good, isn't it?"

It was. I gave the store my almost-new pair of Navy issue 12Bs and walked out in my new pair of 13AAA Bostonians, complete with Odor-Eater insoles.

When I left the store, I walked around downtown San Francisco just looking in the windows and watching the people, thoroughly enjoying myself. On Market Street I saw bunches of sailors and Marines, all in little groups laughing and talking. As I came closer, I could see that they were in front of the USO Club, an organization we had heard about but had never seen; they were just getting started about the time we shipped out.

Out of curiosity—and with nothing else to do—I went inside. Wow, what a layout! Big place, beautifully furnished, and lots of activity. Some of the rooms had pool tables, others were card rooms, and there was a big room—ballroom size—on the far left where an orchestra was playing and couples were dancing. At one end of the room, tables were piled with sandwiches, fruit, cookies, soft drinks, and coffee. I had dinner there that night, a feast right off the snack table. Later, with a couple of Marines whom I had never seen before, we sat and talked to one of the volunteer hostesses. I left about 11:00 and caught a military bus back to the hospital. Don't know what I expected on my first liberty back in civilization, but this one was better than I expected. After all that time in the Pacific, being deprived of the social amenities, hungry much of the time, bombed, shelled, and shot at on a regular basis, burned up and burned out with fevers, it was nice, real nice, to be accepted back in society as a member in good standing.

There Was This Girl...

The next Wednesday, my 30-day sick leave came through; it was to begin on the following Friday, so I took liberty that afternoon and headed for the train station to get the schedule and buy my ticket. The station was a madhouse; hundreds of people crisscrossed that huge interior either arriving, leaving, or going from one train to make connections with another. And there were hundreds more standing in long lines to buy tickets.

That's how I met Helen.

We were standing in this long line, not real sure if this were the right one and not real sure if we were reading the timetable correctly. Standing there and talking a little, we found that we had something in common: We were both from Texas and we were both going to Lubbock — and on the same train! She was going home to Happy, Texas, about 90 miles north of Lubbock. Her final leg would be by bus. She never told me what she was doing in 'Frisco and I didn't ask, but I suspect that she was somewhat unhapy with her job (which had something to do with defense) and or her boyfriend got shipped out. Either or both. An hour later, we had tickets in hand, ready to board Friday at noon. Pullman accommodations were out of the question; the pecking order did not include military enlisted men or civilians unless they had some kind of government priority. It could have been worse; I knew that having a seat on the day coach was far superior to being on a troop transport. I dutifully called home and told the folks which train I would be on and the arrival time.

It was close to 6:00 when we left the train station, my usual chow time. Helen and I had developed a pretty friendly relationship by this time, so I suggested that we go somewhere and have dinner. Fine with her. Any suggestions? She didn't have any, but I had heard a lot about Fisherman's Wharf. Great. We took a bus part of the way, then caught the cable car to the Wharf. The restaurant, suggested the night before at the USO, was nearby; it turned out to be a real winner.

Like many of the restaurants there, it was small but beautifully appointed and had a staff of Italian tuxedo-clad waiters who treated us like royalty. I had not said "Sir" to an officer as many times in the last two years as the waiter called me "Sir" that evening. At that time in the war in late 1943, there wre a lot of GIs around but not many of them wore campaign ribbons. The ones I had earned totaled four, which accounted for the VIP treatment at the restaurant: Better table, outstanding service, and lots of questions about "What's it really like out there?" The question was asked so many times that I finally began telling people what I thought they wanted to hear.

From Fisherman's Wharf we went to a club in one of the big hotels that had a good orchestra and floor show. Don't remember the name, but it was the Mark Hopkins or Saint Anthony, I think.

"Your reservation is in what name, sir?"

I guess my disappointment showed. As we turned to leave, the maitre d' said, "Just a moment, sir. I believe I have just found a cancellation. This way, please."

It was a very good table near the bandstand and the timing was good; the first show was to start in 15 minutes. When the cocktail waitress came, not knowing what to order, I asked Helen what she would like.

"Scotch and soda."

"Make mine the same."

The drinks were served promptly, but the wine steward was with the waitress and asked us for an ID. Helen gave her Texas driver's license; I gave my Navy ID. At age 21, Helen passed; at age 20, I failed. It was embarrassing to be asked to leave, but there was no other recourse. I was damned unhappy. What the hell? I was old enough to pull the kind of duty I had just come from but I still wasn't old enough to buy a beer! The maitre d' was so embarrassed that I felt sort of sorry for him. He told me that they normally didn't let a few months make a difference, but that there was so much Brass present, the wine steward thought it best not to take a chance.

We left.

I took Helen to her apartment. There was a swing on the porch. We sat there and talked — and smooched a little — for the next two hours. She parried my every thrust and countered each suggestion that we go inside. She was pretty good at telling a guy "no" and at the same time keeping his interest up.

Was she pretty? I don't really know and I was in no position to be objective. It had been a year since I had even seen a Caucasian female and this one was the first after all that had time to do as much as hold my hand. I do know that she was tall and slender, had a nice body, and a good personality. But pretty? She might well have looked like ZaSu Pitts, but I was so smitten with her femininity and her attention to me that it really didn't make any difference.

The Train

We met at the station a half-hour before departure time. When they opened the doors, we were among the first aboard and got good seats near the dining car. We were to occupy those seats for the next three days! That's how long it took to travel 1,800 miles. Why so long? There was a war on, gasoline was rationed, the train stopped at every whistle stop on the route, and we were sidetracked half a dozen times a day for troop trains, munitions carriers, etc. — and when the damn train was freewheeling, it never got over 50 miles per hour.

By the time we finished dinner that night, Helen was treating me more like a beau than a one-shot traveling companion. When the lights were turned out about ten that night, she went to sleep with her head on my shoulder — and then I slept with my head on her shoulder. When the train would stop for a sidetrack, we'd smooch a little. By morning we had slept fitfully, smooched off and on, and sneaked a feel now and then. It was an interesting first day.

The second day was pretty much like the first. Actually, it was worse, but we sure did know each other a lot better. We billed and cooed, held hands and smooched, and all things considered, got a lot more interested in each other's physical attributes. Every time the train would stop, I'd go back to the Pullman car and ask the conductor if he had a cancellation. He hadn't, but I was still on his waiting list.

The second night was much worse. We did more smooching and more feeling than we did sleeping. I will say this, everything was done in good taste; we did not make spectacles of ourselves — which was her doing, not mine. (Downtown San Francisco in Union Square would have been okay with me at this point.) When the lights came on in the day coach, we both looked like death warmed over; there were bags under our bloodshot eyes and we both looked like we had a pain for which there was only one prescription.

At breakfast that morning, I was reading the railroad timetable and picked up on something I had missed before. We were due in Lubbock at 3 P.M., but before we arrived there was an hour and a half layover in Hobbs, New Mexico, about 75 miles west of Lubbock. Our train had to wait for a connecting train from the Pacific northwest. Having been in Hobbs before, I knew that there was a big old hotel right in the middle of town, just three city blocks from the depot. We talked about this delay and decided that we owed it to our families to arrive back home fresh and clean. What we would do in Hobbs was to leave the train during the layover, get a room at the hotel so that we could shower and put on fresh clothing, then reboard the train, ready to meet the folks back home. I think Helen was more enthusiastic about the idea than I was—if that's possible. Wow!

It was a very long morning, but the train was on time and the conductor assured me we would utilize all of the scheduled layover. At long last, here came the conductor, going from car to car like a Benedictine monk chanting, "HOBBS NEW MEXICO NEXT STOP." Helen and I were standing at the door, ready to take off for the hotel the minute the porter opened the door.

When I stepped off the train, I thought I was seeing things that weren't there, but they were there: My mother and my sister!! They had made the 75-mile drive from Lubbock to Hobbs to surprise me. They too were thinking about the delay... "So you wouldn't have to worry with that long layover."

It had been a year and a half since I had seen them. I grabbed them and hugged them both while the tears ran freely down my cheeks.

They never knew that those were not tears of joy.

"The best laid plans of mice and men go oft astray..."

Home

All things considered, the 30 days at home were a drag. Seems like a strange thing to say after all those months at sea and in the jungle when all we could think about was getting out of this mess alive and "going home." And here I was, at home, and I really didn't want to be here. I thought about borrowing my sister's car and driving up to Happy, but I didn't. When that "Magic Moment" is gone, I've heard that it's best not to dwell on what might have been; you might miss out on what is yet to come.

Home was not the same. For one thing, I was very angry to learn that my father had been dead for months and I hadn't been told. Nothing seemed right anymore—but somehow I managed to stick it out. I had that funny feeling, kind of a sixth sense, that another attack of fever was on the way, so I got back on Atabrine. I hated that stuff, and so did everyone who had to take it. On the ship coming home, most of us got off all medication, especially Atabrine, because prolonged use turned the skin and eyeballs yellow, exactly like you see in persons who have jaundice. We fearless warriors did not picture ourselves coming home as conquering heroes with yellow skin that looked more Japanese than Caucasian.

There was plenty to do—but not an awful lot that I really wanted to do. I was a guest of and made speeches at Lions, Kiwanis, and the Jaycees. Was even called on to "say a few words" at church one Sunday. Great reception at the American Legion meeting. Dates, the gals were great, but there was something missing. What was missing was yesterday and my adolescence. I had left home such short time ago as a big kid, a high school student, dropout, really—and now I was back but the kid was gone and I wasn't sure I knew, or even wanted to know, the adult who had taken the kid's place.

I made a strange discovery on that leave; I discovered that I couldn't sit through a war movie! Those where the Japs/Germans were shooting at the Americans with rifles and pistols I could handle, almost, but I could not deal with scenes or even newsreels of

147

bombings and shellings. Half the movies made during the war years were patriotic propaganda to some degree and combat was the "in" thing! When the Japs started bombing and shelling William Bendix and John Wayne, I headed for the foxhole before they did. I embarrassed more than one date in that kind of a movie. My friends would laugh, not because it was funny, but because they didn't know what else to do. And I didn't know either.

*   *   *

Each week at home was a month long; I was ready when the time came to board the train for Corpus Christi — which was another memorable day. When I reported in to the Officer of the Day at NAS, Corpus Christi, I was placed under arrest and put in the brig!

The problem was my leave papers from Mare Island: I had not read them so made an assumption that proved to be incorrect. My leave, I knew, was for 30 days; I left on the third of the month and must, therefore, report to Corpus Christi on the third of next month. Correct up to this point. I assumed that I was to report on that date up to midnight, 2400 hours. Incorrect. My orders read "report in not later than 0800 hours...," 8 A.M. I did not read the damned orders when I signed for them because I was much more interested in meeting Helen than examining the details of my last day of leave. The time I reported in was 1700 hours, 5 P.M. The OD did the only thing he was authorized to do. I went to the brig on Friday and I stayed there until Monday morning.

I had never been a prisoner in the brig before, and I'm glad that my stay there was a short term. The OD called in two Marine Military Police. Both wore 45-caliber Colt sidearms; one had a sawed-off shotgun. They placed me in the middle and we marched off to the brig, the Marine with the shotgun bringing up the rear. Before I was put in a cell, I was stripped naked, searched, showered, then given a set of blue dungarees with a big white P painted on the back of the shirt and jacket. Prisoner. Since I had not been placed on bread and water, I was marched with the other prisoners, under armed guard, to and from the chow hall. Embarrassing. And that's all I did Saturday and all day Sunday.

Monday morning at 1100 hours, I was taken from my cell and again marched under guard to the Base Commander's Office for what is called Captain's Mast — a kind of hearing for those with less serious infractions. The captain didn't ask why or if I had anything to say; he said it all. He chewed me out, called me a "combat prima donna," spoke of abusing privileges, and scared the hell out of me. When it was over all I got to say was, "Yes, sir." I was placed on probation for 30 days and sent back to the hospital. No more of the lock-up for me; that was the first and only time in my life that I felt dehumanized; you really have to have been there to know what it feels like to be locked up behind steel bars and have shotgun-armed Marines watch your every move 24 hours a day, like you were a ferocious beast of some kind.

Released from the brig, I reported in to the hospital. In the admitting process, I had to undergo another physical, the results being more positive than the one at Mare Island a little over a month before; heart and blood pressure were still normal, and my weight was up to 122 pounds! The first goal, the doctor said, "is to get your weight up to normal. With your height, you should weigh at least 165 pounds."

They began by putting me on a special "high calorie, high protein" diet. Apparently there were other patients there with a similar problem; we went to a special cafeteria-like chow hall which displayed such an opulent variety of fancy, rich, gourmet foods that even the most demanding of connoisseurs would have been impressed — and they kept a table of snacks laid out for us around the clock in case we felt hungry. I never counted my calorie intake, but it was probably between 5,000 and 10,000 per day. Strip KC sirloin steaks (16 oz. minimum), mashed potatoes buttered and with cream gravy, creamed spinach, avocado salad with bleu cheese dressing, hot apple pie mounded with ice cream. I ate like a field hand and exercised minimally — I walked around the base and swam less than an hour each day.

At the end of the first week, I had gained two pounds.

At the beginning of the second week, I was given insulin shots before each meal. Injected a half hour before mealtime, a certain dosage will make most recipients ravenously hungry — and if food is not taken within the allotted time, then the patient goes into insulin shock, which, I understand, can be quite dangerous, even fatal. Even with the insulin, my appetite did not change appreciably; I was always ravenous and ate like a starving man — with or without insulin.

At the end of 45 days, my weight was up to 125 pounds.

*　　*　　*

I have forgotten what my medical discharge papers said, but I remember malaria and combat fatigue. My physical disability was rated at 40 percent, a rating that helped get my degree from the University of Texas. When I had the sheepskin in hand I requested that the disability be dropped, and it was.

The hospital at NAS Corpus kept me two months, running tests, taking blood samples, and gorging me with food. During this period of confinement, I had no attacks of fever, so the Navy discharged me and sent me home. My weight was up to 129 pounds.

"Home is the sailor, home from the sea..."

*　　　*　　　*

After receiving my discharge papers, I went to work in Dallas in the home office of Southwestern Life Insurance Company, where I learned very quickly that this type of business was not my cup of tea. I quit for one very good reason. It became evident that it was going to take at least a bachelor degree to make it in the highly competitive business field of post–World War II. Business, at that point in time, I though to be my forte. Going back to school was a pretty good deal for the World War II veterans: Books, tuition, and over a hundred bucks a month for living expenses. From Texas Tech, I went to Austin where I earned my bachelor degree at The University of Texas.

But it was at Texas Tech where I met a pretty girl named Jerry Shaw.

"To have and to hold from this day..."

"Baptize you Michael/Patrick, in the name of..."

"Till death us do part..."

*　　　*　　　*

After getting my degree in Business Administration, the job of jobs came along. It started me in sales and led to management; the job took us from a small North Carolina hamlet (where our second son was born) to the British Isles for a year. We then went on to Germany where we spent another five years (there, and all over Europe) before yet another series of events led us to Hawaii. All trails lead to home, so it was back to Dallas in the 1960s.

"The Turbulent Sixties"—and they were turbulent for us. A midlife career change took us to New Haven, Connecticut, to the Episcopal seminary at Yale for three years, ending with a Master's degree in Theology.

The author.

By this time, both sons were in military service; Michael was in the Air Force, Patrick in the Army.

Ordained to the priesthood in 1969, I spent the following 20 years as a professed Churchman, primarily in the parish ministry.

* * *

Mine has been a versatile life and I have liked every bit of it. It hasn't always been a bed of roses, but by and large, most of it has been spent on a positive note.

When I look back over the years to the war, I marvel at the tremendous task accomplished by a non-military democracy in winning a do-or-die war fought by millions of young men and women, most of whom were barely out of their puberty. Winning that conflict could never have been accomplished without the resourcefulness and the sense of humor that turned what could have been a hopeless situation into the biggest challenge this country has ever faced.

I will always be grateful for our military leaders, many of whom were ill-prepared for the task but who led us fearless warriors in such a way that by working together, we met the challenge. We didn't always achieve success, but by damn, we met the challenge! We not only met it, we usually had a pretty good time in the process. And I, personally, appreciate my military superiors who were able to rise over and above their frustration at my antics in stealing peaches, blowing up outhouses, and wrecking jeeps.

The Irish Republican Army sang *The Freedom Song* for many years and ultimately took one of its three-word sentences for its rallying cry: "We shall overcome," a sentence that Martin Luther King, Jr., was later to use quite effectively in his non-violent fight for equality. But long before Martin Luther King, Jr., began his ministry, a rag-tag bunch of sailors on Guadalcanal sang that freedom song, too. And the "we shall overcome" words were prophetic to those of us who had never heard them before, but that is exactly what we did; we overcame hunger, an enemy who outnumbered us in the air, on the sea, and on the ground, and we overcame the pestilence and filth and fear — and in so doing, we did one hell of a good job. I was fortunate indeed to have been a part of it.